THE LANGUAGE OF LITERATURE
General Editor: N. F. Blake
Professor of English Language and Linguistics
University of Sheffield

THE LANGUAGE OF LITERATURE
General Editor: N. F. Blake
Professor of English Language and Linguistics,
University of Sheffield

Published titles

An Introduction to the Language of Literature	N. F. Blake
The Language of Shakespeare	N. F. Blake
The Language of Chaucer	David Burnley
The Language of Wordsworth and Coleridge	Frances Austin
The Language of Irish Literature	Loreto Todd
The Language of D. H. Lawrence	Allan Ingram
The Language of Thomas Hardy	Raymond Chapman
The Language of Drama	David Birch
The Language of Jane Austen	Myra Stokes
The Language of the Metaphysical Poets	Frances Austin
The Language of James Joyce	Katie Wales
The Language of Twentieth-Century Poetry	Lesley Jeffries
The Language of George Orwell	Roger Fowler
The Language of Old and Middle English Poetry	G. A. Lester

Series Standing Order (The Language of Literature)

If you would like to receive future titles in this series as they are published, you can make use of our standing order facility. To place a standing order please contact your bookseller or, in case of difficulty, write to us at the address below with your name and address and the name of the series. Please state with which title you wish to begin your standing order. (If you live outside the United Kingdom we may not have the rights for your area, in which case we will forward your order to the publisher concerned.)

Customer Services Department, Macmillan Distribution Ltd
Houndmills, Basingstoke, Hampshire RG21 6XS, England

An Introduction to the Language of Literature

N. F. BLAKE

MACMILLAN

First published 1990 by
THE MACMILLAN PRESS LTD
Houndmills, Basingstoke, Hampshire RG21 2XS
and London
Companies and representatives
throughout the world

ISBN 0-333-45410-3 hardcover
ISBN 0-333-45411-1 paperback

A catalogue record for this book is available from the British Library.

12	11	10	9	8	7	6	5	4
03	02	01	00	99	98	97	96	95

Printed in Hong Kong

Contents

Preface

In common with the other volumes in the series, this book attempts to explain style in terms which do not presuppose too extensive an acquaintance on the part of the reader with linguistic terminology. In some ways this volume provides the background for many of the others which have appeared or will appear in the series since it is a basic guide to style. Its orientation is not basically theoretical; it attempts to provide help in a pragmatic way for those who recognise the importance of language in literature, but who do not know where to start or how to exploit the particular knowledge and skills they possess. It is hoped that the book will be accessible not only to undergraduates on English and other courses, but also to sixth-formers preparing for the new A level English Language exams. Individual chapters have been delivered in modified forms as lectures to audiences in Britain and elsewhere in Europe. I am grateful to them for their comments and help. An earlier form of the introduction appeared in *Revista Alicantina de Estudios Ingleses* 1 (1988), and I am grateful to its editor for permission to re-use some of that material here.

I have thought it helpful to use mostly the same passages for the various chapters since most readers will be tackling an individual piece of literature in the same way, though there is some variety in the choice of work discussed. I acknowledge permission from Faber & Faber to reproduce the poem, 'This Lunar Beauty', by W. H. Auden.

I would like to thank Barbara Flather and Kath Keegan for their patience and help in the preparation of the typescript.

Sheffield 1989

Introduction

Since Aristotle's time there have been books on the language
of literature, and so one might wonder why another was needed
now. To put this question into perspective one needs to consider
it historically. In classical times the language of literature is en-
compassed in the concept of rhetoric. Originating in Greece as
the art of composing a discourse for the law courts, it gradually
came to embrace all linguistic expression, including literature.
When applied to literature, rhetoric was based around the no-
tion of genre, such as drama, history and lyric. Although rhetoric
involved all aspects of composition, such as the choice of subject
matter and its organisation, it came increasingly to be associated with various figures of speech which were used to embellish
the subject matter of a given genre in an appropriate way. In
the Middle Ages and Renaissance various handbooks on the art
of composition for differing purposes were produced, and these
usually contained long lists of figures and how they were best
deployed. The idea of rhetoric is intimately related to the concept
of the poet as a 'maker', as someone who can learn his or her art
through study and application in much the same way as one could
learn to become a doctor. The handbooks which were produced
were therefore of the same nature as books of grammar, for they
introduced the basic principles with examples of a particular area
of knowledge to enable a student to master that subject.

    All this changed with the onset of Romanticism at the beginning
of the nineteenth century. The role of the poet altered, for the
poet was no longer seen as a maker, but as a seer or prophet
who spoke from the heart. Hence the poet needed a language
which was suitable for this new role. The language had to be
individual, spontaneous and evocative. The rules of rhetoric were
considered too artificial and restrictive, and the older type of
poetic diction suffered a mortal blow from Wordsworth's attack

on it in the preface to the *Lyrical Ballads*. This led to a state of uncertainty and a prolonged period of linguistic experimentation among writers, each of whom had to find his or her own voice since there was no recognised model to follow. Although it took some time to develop, the tendency was for writers to use a style which broke away from the normal grammatical rules of the language so that literary style is today often associated with a language which differs from the norm. This tendency was accentuated by the weakening of the hold of traditional grammar which was felt to place too many restrictions on free expression not only in literature, but also more generally in education. The close link which had existed from classical times between language and literature was severed, and the study of literary language was either not prosecuted very energetically or reduced to the study of the style of individual authors because it was felt that each writer had his or her own style. It was no longer thought that there were general rules of style which could be applied to any writer.

This division was accentuated by the growth of modern linguistics in the twentieth century, for modern linguistics has been concerned both with theoretical aspects of language study and with those varieties of language which have least connection with literature, namely spoken and non-standard varieties. Theoretical studies have focused on more appropriate models for describing English in particular or any language in general. This has meant the abandonment of many of the concepts of traditional grammar, which most literary critics have some understanding of, in favour of a different methodology and terminology which most literary critics are both ignorant and frightened of. More recently linguists have also begun to study language within its social and historical context, an aspect of language study which might have had more intrinsic interest for literary scholars were it not for the fact that criticism has itself moved at the same time more towards a context-free and reader-oriented approach. Practical studies have focused on spoken varieties of language, which by their nature are divorced from literature apart from certain types of oral literature. More importantly the emphasis on the primacy of the spoken variety of language has marginalised literature for linguists, since it is at best simply one other variety available for study.

In the last twenty years or so more attention has been paid to language by literary critics than hitherto. In part this is perhaps because of the inevitable swing of the pendulum away from that form of criticism which ignores language to concentrate on such features as morality, structure and the literariness of literature; and in part it is because those involved with the more theoretical branches of criticism have appreciated that there may be models and methodologies developed within the different schools of linguistics which are applicable to and useful for literary study. This upsurge in interest by critics has presented them with a problem in so far as many are unfamiliar with the techniques and terminology of modern linguistics, for if they have any acquaintance with language study at all it is through traditional grammar. This applies equally to many students in sixth-forms and universities who would like to study the language of their literary texts but do not know how to do so. This need has produced a spate of books and it may be helpful to consider briefly some of the approaches adopted in them.

Most books on stylistics fall into two broad categories: one which provides background information about the topic and draws examples from a wide range of literary texts, and the other which is devoted to a detailed analysis of one or more literary texts by applying a particular linguistic methodology. The first category can naturally be divided into many sub-groups, but two need to be highlighted. The first assumes no linguistic knowledge on the part of the reader and seeks to provide an introduction to linguistic principles, whereas the second assumes some linguistic knowledge and seeks to provide a more general account of the application of linguistic theory to the study of literature.

The authors of those books which assume no linguistic knowledge on the part of the reader find themselves in a dilemma in that they want to explain the application of linguistics to literature and yet within their own terms cannot do so without first explaining what linguistics is. As Cummings and Simmons write in their book, which is one of the better ones of this type: 'Since the means given to the student to describe literary language is the technique of linguistic description, this introduction to literature is also an introduction to the basic tools and basic concerns of linguistic analysis'.[1] In other words the authors assume that the readers have no knowledge of linguistics and cannot easily acquire it for themselves from elsewhere. The reader cannot be trusted to gain the necessary knowledge from the many elementary books on linguistics which are on the market. Hence the book they have written goes through phonology and phonetics, graphology, grammar, lexis and context in much the same way as any standard grammar of the language would. It would not be surprising if many readers of this book thought that more attention is given to basic grammatical tools than to their application to literary texts, even though the examples are all drawn from such texts. The approach is dictated by linguistic models and every aspect of the sentence is expounded at some length. It is assumed that all this information is necessary, though it is questionable, for example, whether a high level of phonetic knowledge is essential for the reading of literary texts, however desirable it may be. The detail provided may be too much for most readers, who may abandon such books because they will feel they are being taught linguistics rather than stylistics.

It is also characteristic of such books that they provide a modern methodology, based usually on systemic linguistics or transformational generative linguistics, for it is accepted in such books that modern stylistics must involve a modern linguistic methodology and terminology. Their intention is to provide a grammatical basis for literary analysis, not to discuss what linguistic knowledge might be most suitable for the critic. Since most critics are more likely to have some knowledge of traditional grammar, it might be thought that a linguistic approach to literature which exploited that knowledge was more suitable for most critics. Teaching a completely new methodology may simply alienate those one is trying to reach. Modern grammars have two disadvantages when they are applied to literary texts. Traditional grammars are word based and proceed from word classes to the make-up of sentences. Modern grammars are sentence based and divide any sentence into the functional elements which compose it. Students often find vocabulary the most interesting part of language study and authors themselves often present their composition process as a struggle with words. A grammatical model which places emphasis on sounds and syntax as against lexis may not meet with much response from the reader. It is also the case that modern grammars have usually been constructed to analyse the spoken language precisely because traditional grammar was thought to be too closely linked with the standard written variety. Although modern grammars have subsequently been applied to the written language as well, many of them are predicated on having access to an unlimited corpus of information such as one would find in contemporary language situations. But most literary language is of necessity language of the past and some of it can be from a fairly distant past. The material available for comparative linguistic purposes may be slight, and it may be difficult to apply some of the techniques of linguistic analysis to the extant pieces. Stylistic studies of earlier literature are sometimes available using a traditional grammatical framework. It may be difficult to align these with investigations conducted on modern linguistic terms, and so the benefit of the earlier work will be lost. Consequently although books of this type are designed as elementary handbooks, users are uncertain how to apply the information they contain because they seem so remote from what they know already and because there seems to be no convenient point of entry.

Those books which assume some knowledge of linguistics usually accept that readers have some grasp of the grammatical make-up of the sentence, and so in discussions of the relationship between language and literature they often deal principally with units bigger than the sentence, an aspect of language study which has grown considerably in recent years. Pragmatics, cohesion and discourse analysis bulk large in such books, although many of the basic tenets of these areas of study can be understood even by those who have little knowledge of units smaller than the sentence. The approach of books of this kind is usually theoretical, even though it is supported by detailed analysis of particular passages. The discussions of general principle often overlap with theoretical approaches proposed by literary critics, and for some writers there is no doubt that the primary purpose of such books is a rapprochement between linguistic and critical theories. Consequently books of this type are rather less uniform in their presentation. Books seeking to introduce linguistics as part of the study of style follow the pattern of formal grammars, precisely because such information is susceptible to formal presentation. Beyond a sentence, there are fewer formal rules, and this makes it difficult for scholars seeking to base their approach to style on these concepts to present a coherent body of knowledge. As Anthony Easthope explains:

Linguistics, the science which takes language as its object, can show how an utterance takes its place in the system of language at levels up to and including the sentence. It cannot show how and why one sentence connects with another into a cohesive whole: this is a matter of discourse. . . . Discourse, then, is a term which specifies the way that sentences form a consecutive order, take part in a whole which is homogeneous as well as heterogeneous.[2]

It is not surprising that the title of Easthope's book is *Poetry as Discourse*, though he makes it clear that since the pattern formed by consecutive sentences can be both heterogeneous as well as homogeneous it is difficult to present a coherent set of rules which may be applied to a given literary text.

It could be said that, because books of this kind operate at a rather more theoretical level than those inculcating linguistic knowledge as a prelude to style, they presuppose some familiarity with basic linguistic concepts and a degree of sophistication in critical practice. They tend not to be practical handbooks showing how a student might analyse a particular passage, for they take all literature as their subject matter and seek to show how the application of some linguistic ideas can help to a greater understanding of it. Consequently such books might be said to belong to the second tier of books on stylistics: they are extremely valuable in outlining general theory, but less helpful to someone trying to grapple with the language of a text.

The other broad category of books about style consists of those which contain analyses of particularly literary works without necessarily explaining the philosophical or theoretical background of their approach. Inevitably such analyses will differ in what linguistic model they use and in how much detail they provide. At one end of the scale are those books which provide a detailed linguistic inventory of the text being analysed, of which the best example is probably *Shakespeare's Verbal Art in Th'Expence of Spirit* by Jakobson and Jones.[3] Although only a brief book, it attempts to provide a complete account of all the linguistic features in that Shakespearian sonnet – or at least all those which the authors considered significant. In fact, some of the features, such as rhyme, are not exclusively linguistic. This book looks at the structure of the poem and relates that structure to grammatical features, though these details are stated to exist rather than evaluated for their critical significance. For example it is claimed that:

Within each of the two contiguous strophic pairs, anterior/posterior, grammatical contrasts between neighboring strophes play an incomparably wider role (odd *versus* even and outer *versus* inner) than specific similarities in their grammatical structure.

(p. 25)

Many readers may find it difficult to exploit this system elsewhere and some may even feel that even in this example the opposition of grammatical features is something which the system demands rather than a help to understanding the organisation of the poem. There is too much information, not all of which is relevant to a critical understanding of the text. Furthermore the approach adopted in this text is suitable only for poetry since it refers to so many exclusively poetic features such as rhyme and strophic structure.

At the other end of the scale are those books which contain essays by different people, each of which is devoted to the analysis of a single text through focusing on a particular linguistic feature in that text. These essays approach their texts in widely differing ways, not only in methodology but also in what linguistic feature may be worth exploring. The best-known single essay is probably Halliday's analysis of passages in Golding's *The Inheritors*.[4] This essay explores the transitivity system in the novel. Halliday raises the important question of relevance in the application of linguistic tools to literature:

This, it seems to me, is one of the central problems in the study of 'style in language': I mean the problem of distinguishing between mere linguistic regularity, which in itself is of no interest to literary studies, and regularity which is significant for the poem or prose work in which we find it.

(p. 325)

He implies that the application of language methodology to literature must be through isolated linguistic features and not through blanket coverage as provided in the book by Jakobson and Jones. This does raise the problem as to how one recognises a 'regularity which is significant for the poem or prose work'. Those who subject a text to a total linguistic analysis have no problem in that they apply the teaching of a formal grammar to a text in every aspect; their difficulty is in deciding how much of the information provided in this way is relevant. If, on the other hand, one is looking only for significant linguistic features, it could be argued that those with no experience of these matters will not easily be able to distinguish what is significant from what is not, whereas for those with experience the detailed analysis may not be necessary at all since they will have arrived at their conclusions without going through the process of analysis. To some extent it may be that one will decide to investigate a particular linguistic feature in a text on the basis of a hunch, which is inspired by one's experience as a reader. Although this may be so, it provides little consolation for those with little literary or linguistic sophistication for they are unlikely to have the hunches which can be tested by a detailed linguistic analysis. Consequently those who read books of this kind may well be impressed by the erudition and critical response of the analyst but uncertain how they should emulate him.

This brief survey is not intended to indicate that these various books are lacking in usefulness or critical acumen, but simply to reveal that there is a gap in what is available at present about the language of literature. It is self-evident that anyone studying the language of literature has to know something about linguistics, though we have probably got to a stage where we can assume that that information is readily available from other sources for those who want to acquire it. But a high level of linguistic knowledge is not necessary for most purposes, and this is where one of the problems in methodology and approach originates. Modern linguistics is not a homogeneous subject, for there are different linguistic models available, and those who promote one often try to denigrate the others. It is difficult for those not in linguistics to know what model to follow. In this matter one needs to be pragmatic. Most critics and students are likely to know something of traditional grammar and so any linguistic theory which builds on that knowledge is likely to be easier for non-specialists to use. In this book I shall follow the methodology outlined in my *Traditional English Grammar and Beyond*, which takes its point of departure from traditional grammar and which does not go too far into theoretical discussions.[5] However, all linguistic features which are used in this book will be briefly described, though those that want a fuller explanation in linguistic terms may find it in my previous one.

Another problem concerns the scope of any linguistic investigation. Modern study of language divides into several branches. What most people understand by 'grammar' is the make-up of individual sentences, that is the units such as noun and verb or subject and object which together form a complete sentence. However, as I have already indicated, modern scholarship has also tackled the way in which sentences are linked together to form a coherent piece of discourse. What are the links which allow us to understand two consecutive sentences to form a unified utterance, basically to make sense? It may be appreciated that in some twentieth-century literature, particularly drama, this may be an important consideration. Linguists have also given considerable attention recently to language in context within differing social situations. This is something which has had less impact on the study of language in literature, because literature is often regarded as being less context-oriented than many other varieties of language. To these varieties of linguistic concern one can add the problems that spring from literature itself which not only consists of various genres like poetry, prose and drama, but also represents what has been written in these genres over the last thousand years or more. It is not very probable that the way to examine the language of a novel would also be the most appropriate way to examine the language of a play. Equally the best approach to a poem from Chaucer's time may not be the best method to adopt for a contemporary one. The point of entry for a linguistic study of a piece of literature may vary according to what category it belongs to. It is not possible for a book of this size to be comprehensive.

Since most readers of this book are more likely to have some familiarity with the grammatical make-up of a sentence, it is best to start with that side of language study before moving on later in the book to consider aspects of language beyond the sentence. Within the sentence one could start with sounds, spellings, words or syntax. The first two are not likely to be considered so important by most readers, partly because silent reading from modernised editions is today the commonest literary experience. Readers and writers often find words the most absorbing part of the language of literature, but the study of words does have some problems. There are fewer general rules which apply to words as compared with syntax, and considerable historical knowledge or access to historical dictionaries is desirable to provide the necessary background information against which to evaluate the words in a given text. I shall therefore commence our investigation of the language of literature by examining the syntax of the sentence before going on to words and other elements of sentence make-up. The other problem concerns the texts to use as examples. In the early parts of the book I will not use dramatic texts because of some of the special linguistic characteristics they exhibit, but they are useful as illustrations of some elements of language beyond the sentence and will be called on then. I have thought it sensible to use only poetry and prose in the earlier chapters of this book. Furthermore, it seems appropriate to use the same texts for illustrative purposes in each chapter so that there is some link between the chapters and no suggestion that the examples have been chosen specifically to illustrate a particular linguistic feature. It is desirable for such an example to be short and reasonably familiar, and I have chosen Shakespeare's Sonnet 129. This sonnet is brief because sonnets have only fourteen lines; it is by an author known to everybody; it is also the sonnet used by Jakobson and Jones in their book referred to earlier. It has the advantage of being an older text, for it is wrong to create the impression that a study of the language of literature is concerned only with contemporary texts. However, each chapter will also be illustrated with examples drawn from other texts, and these will often be in prose and more modern than the Shakespearian sonnet.

1 Sentence Structure

In analysing the language of a literary text it is important to have a point of entry into that text, and as suggested in the Introduction the best place to start is with syntax since this leads straight to the heart of a text by exposing its structure. This type of approach should give further leads to follow in the analysis. The structure may be looked at in three ways: the clause elements which go to make up each sentence; the presentation of the content in theme/rheme and topic/comment formats; and the wider organisation of each sentence into declarative, interrogative or imperative patterns. Each of these needs a brief explanation before we proceed to the analysis of particular texts.

Each sentence consists of clause elements, of which in English there are five. They are subject, predicator, object, complement and adjunct. Not every sentence will contain all elements, but most sentences will contain at least a subject and predicator (for only imperative sentences dispense with the subject) and the majority will actually have more than these two elements. As there are only five possible elements, it should not take much expertise to break any sentence down into its constituent parts. The *subject* represents who or what performs the action of the verb; the *predicator* is the verb which is performed by the subject; the *object* suffers the action of the verb and is a person or thing which is different from the subject; the *complement* is like the object but it is identical with or refers to the subject; and the *adjunct* is anything which fails to fit into the previous four categories and usually answers to one of the questions Where? When? or How? In a sentence such as *The postman left the parcel behind the dustbin*, there is a subject *The postman*, a predicator *left*, an object *the parcel*, and an adjunct *behind the dustbin*. Complements and objects do not normally occur together, because each tends to be associated with a different kind of verb; complements, for example, occur with verbs like the verb *to be*. So in the sentence *He is a postman*, we have a subject *He*, a predicator *is*, and a complement *a postman*.

For the purpose of this type of analysis theme and rheme may be accepted in the following way. The theme is the first clause element in any sentence, and the rheme is the rest of the sentence without the theme. It is also possible to separate the final element in any sentence and say that it exhibits end-focus. As a general principle it may be said that the subject of most English sentences is likely to be in the theme position, but naturally in literature this combination may be broken. This is because what occurs as theme in most sentences is likely to receive emphasis, and one way to give some element emphasis which it would not normally have is to put it at the head of the sentence. Equally the end of a sentence carries more stress than the middle of a sentence, which is why the concept of end-focus is used. But end-focus is not such a prominent feature as thematic emphasis. In the sentence *The postman left the parcel on the doorstep*, the subject *The postman* is in the theme position and hence its stress is restricted because the sentence conforms to a standard pattern. If the sentence were to be rewritten as *On the doorstep the postman left the parcel*, then the theme position is occupied by *On the doorstep* which because it breaks the normal sentence pattern has considerable emphasis. Indeed, to many speakers of the language the sentence might almost seem unnatural because of this rearrangement of the elements, but it reflects an order which is not uncommon in literary texts. Whereas deciding what is the theme in a sentence is relatively straightforward, since it refers to the first element in the sentence, this is not true of topic, which may be defined as the psychological subject of a sentence. It is what the sentence is really about – the focal point of the sentence to which the rest acts as some elaboration or comment. It may on occasion be difficult to decide what is the topic; or rather one reader may disagree with another. For example, if you put a sentence like *The car hit the man* into its passive form *The man was hit by the car*, the subject is clearly different in each case. It may not be so self-evident that the topic has also changed with the new structure.

Each sentence has a structure which reflects the type of utterance intended by the speaker. Three structures are recognised in English: declarative which is when a statement is made; interrogative which reflects a question; and imperative which introduces a command. The first type has subject-predicator order, the second predicator-subject, and the third predicator only. In the latter two cases the predicator would normally come in the theme position, and when that is so the predicator would not carry additional stress because of that position. A possible fourth type, the exclamatory sentence, in which the object or complement is put first is best seen as a sub-type of the declarative sentence since the subject still comes before the predicator.

It is time now to turn to the application of these principles against Sonnet 129. The sonnet is reproduced here as it is printed in the first quarto of 1609 except that I have emended *Made* to *Mad* at the beginning of line 9. Line numbers have been added for ease of reference:

1   TH'expence of Spirit in a waste of shame
2   Is lust in action, and till action, lust
3   Is periurd, murdrous, blouddy full of blame,
4   Sauage, extreame, rude, cruell, not to trust,
5   Inioyd no sooner but dispised straight,
6   Past reason hunted, and no sooner had
7   Past reason hated as a swollowed bayt,
8   On purpose layd to make the taker mad.
9   Mad In pursut and in possession so,
10 Had, hauing, and in quest to haue extreame,
11 A blisse in proofe and proud and very wo,
12 Before a ioy proposd behind a dreame,
13 All this the world well knowes yet none knowes well,
14 To shun the heauen that leads men to this hell.

Immediately one recognises that there are only two sentences in this sonnet, the first from line 1 to line 8, and the second occupying the last six lines. Each sentence can itself be divided into two parts. The first sentence is divided into two clauses by the *and* in line 2, so that the first clause consists of one and a half lines and the second of six and a half lines. The second sentence is divided into two clauses by the *yet* in line 13 so that its first clause consists of four and a half lines and its second of one and a half lines. Even this basic division into sentences and independent clauses reveals a structure in the sonnet, for it begins and ends with a clause of one and a half lines.

Two lengthy clauses occupy the middle section of the sonnet so that there is a mirror image of short + long set against long + short clauses. However, this understanding does not take us very far in analysing the poem, and it is time to turn to the make-up of the clauses themselves.

The first clause is relatively simple consisting as it does of a simple subject, predicator, complement (SPC) structure.[1] This means taking *TH'expence of Spirit in a waste of shame* as S and *lust in action* as C; the P is the simple *is*. In this case the subject also acts as the theme; whether it is also the topic is more difficult to determine as is frequently the case in those sentences with a verb *to be*. For the present it may be more appropriate to accept that *lust in action* is the topic since that seems to be the focal point of the clause, and indeed of the sonnet as a whole. The next clause, which follows the link word *and*, has a similar structure except that it has an adjunct (A) at the beginning resulting in the order ASPC. Clearly there has been an attempt to make the two clauses of this sentence imitate and contrast with each other. In the second line to produce a mirror image of *lust in action*, it was necessary for Shakespeare to put the prepositional group before the noun and that automatically transformed it into an adjunct as distinct from a part of the complement. Equally whereas *lust in action* forms the complement of the first clause, *lust* is the subject of the second one. The subject of the first clause is rather longer than its complement, whereas the complement in the second clause is very much longer than its subject. In the second clause the theme is *till action*, but *lust* is both the subject and the topic. Placing *till action* in the theme position makes this clause appear more active than might otherwise be the case because it contains a stative verb *is*, which implies description rather than action. Both clauses are declaratives, and the overall effect of the sentence is to suggest a pattern which can be described thematically as 'a is b and b is a'. When stated in this way the theme of the poem may seem trite, but its development makes it very different from that bald statement. In the second clause the complement is very long for it stretches over more than six lines. This arrangement is dictated in part by the needs of the sonnet as a whole since the second sentence mirrors the first; and this in turn helps to explain why the first clause in the first sentence did not thematise the topic. The overall structure of the sonnet demands that the first topic should occur in the complement position. Equally it is improbable that a poet would open his poem with a long introductory theme which is not the topic of the poem, and so it is hardly surprising that the initial theme is relatively brief. At present our concern is with the general structure of the poem, and so the make-up of the individual elements will be left till later.

The second sentence is divided into two clauses like the first, but the pattern of division is not identical in that the first clause of the second sentence is very long, extending as it does to over four lines. This clause starts off with a long object, because the verb in this clause is one which takes an object rather than a complement. The bulk of this object precedes what might be called its summation in the *All this*, which represents the core of the object. The structure of this opening clause is OSAP, with the O as a very long element and the other three represented by one or two words. The second clause in this sentence is separated from the first by the conjunction *yet*, which although it is a co-ordinating conjunction is rather more adversative than the *and* which linked the two clauses in the first sentence. This contrastive function is accentuated by the subjects of each clause, since *the world* (i.e. everybody) as the first subject is set in direct contrast with *none* (i.e. nobody) as the second subject. This contrast is heightened because the predicators in each clause are identical, namely *knowes*, and the adjunct *well* is also repeated. The second clause has the structure SPAO. In this clause the subject *none* is the theme, and the emphasis which this throws on *none* in the final clause of the sonnet makes the sonnet finish on a somewhat pessimistic note. The topic of this final clause is the object of the clause *to shun the heauen that leads men to this hell*; and it may be suggested that the final word *hell* carries end-focus, not only because it is accentuated through the rhyme. The last line also carries a contrast between *heauen* and *hell*, which forces these two words into greater prominence and so makes the end-focus on *hell* even more telling. It may be worth noting now that the object in this final clause has a rather different structure from the other object and complements of the sonnet in that it contains a relative clause with its own SPOA structure. The other object and complements contain only non-finite verbs, either participles or infinitives, and so appear to be more static and descriptive. This final object contains the relative clause, which has a predicator which is an active verb highly suggestive of movement. Hence it allows the sonnet to finish on a much more active note, and that in turn adds to the end-focus on *hell*, which is seen in relation to that active verb. It may also be suggested that the end-focus on *hell* links back with the opening theme *TH'expence of Spirit in a waste of shame*, and together they encapsulate the message of the sonnet. The initial theme is shown to lead to the final end-focus. Neither is the topic of a sentence or indeed of the sonnet as a whole, for in the first sentence the clauses have identical topics, namely *lust in action* and *lust*. In the second sentence the topics are more difficult to determine, but they appear to be the objects rather than the subjects.

Each sentence and each clause in the sonnet is declarative. This makes it appear as though the sonnet proceeds by a series of statements which are self-evidently true because they are almost presented as *obiter dicta*. There is no discussion or questioning of these statements. They represent facts which appear to be eternally true.

Even by undertaking such a straightforward analysis as this one which looks at the major structural devices in the poem, one begins to come to some understanding of the organisation and presentation of the material and to gain some insight into other features that might be looked at. There are in the sonnet two long clauses in the middle, each of which is long because it contains either an extended complement or an extended object. This suggests that this kind of clause element needs further analysis, and that we shall come to in the next chapter. In addition there seem to be some words like *lust*, *heauen* and *hell* which are key ones in the poem, and the choice and exploitation of the lexis in English is another feature that needs to be looked at more thoroughly; and this will be the subject of a following chapter.

In the mean time it may be appropriate to examine a piece of prose along the same general lines used to tackle the sonnet, and I have chosen the opening of Jane Austen's *Mansfield Park*. I have introduced a number at the head of each sentence for ease of reference.

(1) About thirty years ago, Miss Maria Ward of Huntingdon, with only seven thousand pounds, had the good luck to captivate Sir Thomas Bertram, of Mansfield Park, in the county of

Northampton, and to be thereby raised to the rank of a baronet's lady, with all the comforts and consequences of an handsome house and large income. (2) All Huntingdon exclaimed on the greatness of the match, and her uncle, the lawyer, himself, allowed her to be at least three thousand pounds short of any equitable claim to it. (3) She had two sisters to be benefited by her elevation; and such of their acquaintance as thought Miss Ward and Miss Frances quite as handsome as Miss Maria, did not scruple to predict their marrying with almost equal advantage. (4) But there certainly are not so many men of large fortune in the world, as there are pretty women to deserve them. (5) Miss Ward, at the end of half a dozen years, found herself obliged to be attached to the Rev. Mr Norris, a friend of her brother-in-law, with scarcely any private fortune, and Miss Frances fared yet worse. (6) Miss Ward's match, indeed, when it came to the point, was not contemptible, Sir Thomas being happily able to give his friend an income in the living of Mansfield, and Mr and Mrs Norris began their career of conjugal felicity with very little less than a thousand a year.

It would be agreeable to prolong this quotation to the end of the paragraph but what is there should be sufficient for our purpose.

The sentences in this passage are all declarative, and that is what one might expect for the opening of a novel where description is the order of the day as the novelist sketches in the background before embarking on the narration. However, the description is by no means neutral in its presentation, and the tone it conveys depends upon the organisation of the individual sentences. When these are examined, it is apparent that the majority of the sentences consist of two co-ordinating clauses linked by *and*. Although the fourth sentence also divides into two parts, its structure is somewhat different from that of the other sentences, a fact which is emphasised by the *But* which introduces it. The first sentence does not consist of two co-ordinate clauses, but it does have a parallel structure within it for the object contains two qualifiers linked by *and* dependent upon it: *to captivate* and *to be thereby raised* both depend upon *luck*. This structure suggests that parallelism and contrast may well form important attributes of the passage, since dualism is a feature of all the opening sentences of the novel. The sentences are in general not long, and their structure is not particularly elaborate as we shall see; what is more significant is how the various elements within the sentences are arranged.

The opening sentence has a relatively simple structure of ASPO; it commences with the adjunct *About thirty years ago*. This is not altogether unusual since many narratives open with an adjunct such as *Once upon a time*. This adjunct is the theme of the sentence, but it is not the topic, which is *Miss Maria Ward*. The adjunct, which is one of time, distances the story and suggests that if we are to understand the present we first have to come to realise what happened in the past. The topic is *Miss Maria Ward*, as already noted, and this could indicate that she is to be the heroine of the story or certainly the main subject of the rest of the paragraph. It turns out, though, that she is simply one of three sisters, and she is the one against whom the other two will be evaluated. As the significant facts given about this lady are her county of origin and her annual income, we deduce that birth and money are important considerations in any marriage arrangement. Because Miss Maria Ward is the topic and subject of this sentence, it appears that the role of women is more important than that of men, and that in her own case it was she who captivated her future husband rather than he who took the initiative; it is women who are probably going to be at the centre of this novel. The amount of Miss Maria Ward's annual income is set into perspective by the final words of the sentence *an handsome house and large income*, which are in end-focus and emphasise the concept of money in marriage. The consequences of a good match are a comfortable life.

The second sentence has a parallel structure, for it contains two declarative statements, each of which is made up of an SPO structure. However, the grammatical subject of each clause, and hence the theme in each case, is not what one might have expected, for the topics in these two clauses are the greatness of the match and the insufficient claim that Miss Maria Ward had on it. The bystanders of the match, as it were, have been made into the grammatical subjects and theme, with the result that the emphasis falls upon the impact that this match had upon those in the immediate family circle and vicinity. Hence *All Huntingdon* and *her uncle, the lawyer, himself*, are thematised; in these two subjects the inclusion of both *all* and *himself* helps to underline the width and depth of the response which is reported. This allows both *greatness of the match* and *short of any equitable claim to it* to have end-focus, and in this way to continue the link with the previous sentence since the end-focus in that sentence is on the consequences and comforts of a great match, namely *an handsome house and large income.* The position of money is thus kept firmly before the reader through the organisation of the clause elements.

The third sentence is divided into two parts, though in this case they are separated by a semi-colon. The subject of the first clause is *She,* i.e. Miss Maria Ward, and of the second *such of their acquaintance as thought Miss Ward and Miss Frances quite as handsome as Miss Maria.* These two clauses pick up the first two sentences, for the first sentence has Miss Maria Ward as its subject, and the second has her neighbours and relatives. The two sisters are not in themselves the subject, theme or even topic of this sentence, and so they are introduced somewhat obliquely. It is not as though they are presented to the reader in their own right, but as though their only interest is as sisters to Miss Maria Ward. The fortunate marriage of one sister has set a yardstick for the other sisters to emulate, and that emulation is naturally in the quality of the marriages which they can obtain. It has already been made clear that that quality is measured in financial terms, and this is emphasised further in this sentence by the elements which are in end-focus in these clauses, for the use of the semi-colon after the first clause enables its final element to have greater end-focus than would have been the case with a comma or no punctuation mark at all. The two elements in end-focus are *her elevation* and *almost equal advantage.* They are directly related to each other, and they keep alive the sense of benefit (i.e. financial advantage) to be made by a good marriage.

The fourth sentence opens with *But,* which here has the nature of an adjunct setting a contrastive relationship with what has preceded. This sentence falls into two parts, each with an SPC structure, and their similarity in structure is emphasised by the fact that each part has *there are* as its SP. This puts the complement in each part into focus, and naturally they tend to form a pair so that *men of large fortune* and *pretty women to deserve them* are closely associated. There is thus set up a close link between beauty and financial reward, which develops the idea characteristic of the paragraph hitherto in that beauty as such has not been made a condition of a good marriage so far except through the word *handsome* in relation to the two sisters. Now it is implied that it is simply in relation to their beauty that women deserve good marriages. The *in the world* which is part of the first complement continues the undercurrent of exaggeration introduced by the *all* in *All Huntingdon*.

The fifth sentence continues the parallel structure of the rest of the paragraph, dealing as it does first with one of the remaining two sisters and then with the other. Hitherto the sisters have been treated as equal in their expectations; now it is revealed that their fortunes reflect their seniority. One sister had done very well for herself; another has done reasonably satisfactorily; but the third has done very badly. This sentence is in two parts with Miss Ward as the first subject, and Miss Frances as the second subject. In order to make this parallelism of subjects and themes more forceful, the adjunct *at the end of half a dozen years* is put in second position in the sentence. This contrasts with the opening sentence where the adjunct was in first position, though in that sentence there is only the one subject and so there is no need to thematise it in the same way. Each clause exhibits end-focus, *with scarcely any private fortune* in the first and *worse* in the second. These elements continue the emphasis on the financial aspects of marriage for it is clear that *worse* means marrying someone with no private fortune at all. Equally the parallelism between the two clauses is notable for the uneven length of each, for the first clause is much longer than the second. There is an implication here that the youngest sister does not need many words spent on her because she married so badly, as though the financial condition of each marriage is reflected in the number of words the author bestows on its participants.

Naturally the sixth sentence goes on to offer some comment on the marriage of Miss Ward, which is shown not to be so disastrous after all. The sentence again falls into two parts linked by *and*. The subject and theme of the first one are Miss Ward's match. This organisation contrasts with that found in the second sentence, where the greatness of Miss Maria Ward's match is made the complement, for the theme is *All Huntingdon*. This contrast implies that no one bothered to exclaim on the greatness of this second marriage. Indeed this sixth sentence resembles in the organisation of its first part that of the previous sentence, for the subject is followed in each case by an adjunct. In first case it was *at the end of half a dozen years* and in the second both *indeed* and *when it came to the point*. This separation of subject and predicator suggests deliberation followed by resignation; it was the best that could be achieved. This is reinforced by the *thousand a year* in end-focus, which continues the idea of money in marriage so prominent in the passage as a whole. It is considerably less than the other sums mentioned, but it is held out as a sufficiency.

It could be said that the topic of most sentences in this passage is marriage and the financial rewards that come from a good marriage. It is not often that either is made the subject or theme of the individual sentences, though Miss Ward's match is the topic of the final sentence. This separation of topic and theme is one way in which Jane Austen is able to build up the ironic tone of the passage, because it is implied that the passage is dealing thematically with the facts of the sisters' marriages, whereas what is really at stake is what they expect to get out of marriage and how they expect to be financially rewarded for their beauty. The financial implications of the marriages are brought into end-focus, and this underlines the real purpose of marriage, which is not brought out in the thematisation of the basic narrative.

The analysis of these opening sentences of *Mansfield Park* reinforces what we discovered from Sonnet 129. Even breaking down the sentences in a literary text into their clause elements helps to provide insights into the structure and tone of the work. It also suggests further ways in which an analysis could be pursued; and this is something to which we shall turn in the next chapter.

2   Group Structure: The Noun Group

In the previous chapter we looked at the make-up of sentences, which can be broken down into their constituent elements of subject, predicator, object, complement and adjunct. Each of these elements can be represented by a group of words, such as a noun group, adjective group, verb group, adverb group or prepositional group. Of these the noun group is perhaps the most important in English sentences because of its make-up and role; and this chapter will be devoted to a consideration of the noun group to which the adjective group is very closely allied. We may begin by considering its formation.

A noun group may be recognised as such because it consists of one or more words which can act as the subject of a sentence. Not all noun groups are the subject of a sentence, but if a group of words could act as the subject of a sentence, it will form a noun group. A noun group consists of up to five elements, only one of which, the head, is an obligatory element. All the other elements are dependent upon the head and refer to it in some way. Consider, for example, the group *The handicapped girl in the wheel-chair*. It may be appreciated that this group could act as the subject of a sentence by the addition of something like *is homesick*, and consequently it is a noun group. In this particular group it is not too difficult to understand that *girl* is the word upon which the other words in the group depend. It is the word which cannot be removed without making nonsense of the remaining words. Most of the other words could easily be removed and still leave a group which makes good sense. Thus to omit *handicapped* would leave *The girl in the wheel-chair*, and to omit *in the wheel-chair* would leave *The handicapped girl*. The head of a noun group is usually a noun, as in this case. In some sentences where the noun group consists of a single word, the head may be a pronoun such as *he* or *she*.

In the group given as an example in the last paragraph there are words both before and after the head, but these words fall into different patterns. As a general rule the words before the head are single ones, which are independent of one another; whereas those after the head form phrases or small units which hang together. The unit *in the wheel-chair* forms a set of interdependent words which must be treated as a whole. You can include or omit all the words, but you cannot leave out only one or two of them. This difference between the words which precede and those which follow the head can be important in deciding which is the head of a noun group. This can pose problems in that it is possible to make adjectives, adverbs and verbs into nouns, as well as nouns into adjectives. The latter is frequent, and then the order of the words in a group is of particular significance. The following groups are perfectly admissible in English: *a system analysis* and *an analysis system*. Here two identical words appear in two orders; each order means something different. As single words precede the head in a noun group, it follows that in *system analysis* the head is *analysis*, and in *analysis system* the head is *system*. It is this understanding of English word order which enables us to make sense of complicated headlines in newspapers such as *power enquiry report fiasco*.

Two different kinds of words can appear before the head of a noun group, and they are called determiner and modifier. The latter corresponds closely, but not entirely, with adjectives in traditional grammar. The difference between a determiner and a modifier can be seen in the example already given: *The handicapped girl in the wheel-chair*. The head is *girl*, the modifier is *handicapped*, and the determiner is *the*. Determiners belong to a closed class of words, that is there is a finite number of them, and each word is mutually incompatible, that is you cannot have two words in the same class following each other. The determiners consist of words which in traditional grammar are classified in such categories as article, possessive adjective, demonstrative adjective or interrogative adjective. *The* and *my*, for example, are mutually incompatible, for if there is one it is not possible to have the other: *the my book* is not a permissible group in English. Modifiers on the other hand belong to an open class of word, and new modifiers can be invented at the drop of a hat, as witness *system* and *analysis* in the preceding paragraph. In principle it is possible to have as many modifiers as one wants before a head, but in practice it is unusual to have more than three. The example *power enquiry report fiasco* is close to the limit of what is acceptable. Modifiers belong to different categories, and normally this categorisation affects the order in which modifiers appear. *The big white drum* is a more acceptable order than *the white big drum*, for adjectives of colour come after adjectives of quality and size. Adjectives which have been formed from nouns come near the head of the group, so that *the elegant period houses* is preferred to *the period elegant houses*. As can be appreciated, all these modifiers are single words which are independent of the other modifiers in the group. But some modifiers may have their character altered through an intensifier such as *very*. One can speak of *a very big, white drum*, or even *a big, very white drum*. The *very* refers to the modifier and not to the head, for it could not be *a very drum*. The use of intensifiers is one of those few instances in which a modifier consists of more than a single word.

The head is followed by a unit consisting of more than one word in standard English. An expression like *the house white* (which contains a single word after the head) is not acceptable today, though it was possible in some earlier varieties of the language and may still be found in some forms of poetic language. The unit which follows the head in a noun group is now referred to as a qualifier, though the term post-modifier may also be encountered. Because qualifiers consist of more than a single word, they fall into many different types and it is difficult to categorise them fully here. The most common types are probably as follows. First is the prepositional phrase, which consists of a preposition and a noun phrase such as *in the wheel-chair*. Second is the relative clause, which is a clause introduced usually by a subject which is a relative pronoun and followed by a predicator and other sentence elements. An example of this type of qualifier is *The handicapped girl who is in the wheel-chair*, in which *who is in the wheel-chair* forms the qualifier which is a clause consisting of subject *who*, predicator *is*, and adjunct *in the wheel-chair*. Third is the qualifier which is in apposition to the head; usually this apposition consists of a noun phrase which could by reversing the order in the noun group have formed its head. Hence the group *Mr Smith the postman* contains the head *Smith* and a qualifier *the postman*. But the group could be rewritten as *the postman Mr Smith*, in which *postman* is the head and *Mr Smith* is a qualifier in apposition. This type of qualifier is common in poetic language, in which the phrases in apposition often add to the metaphorical and symbolic meaning of the poem. Fourth is the use of adjectives after the noun, which is possible when there are two or three linked by *and*. A group like *The house, white and silent*, is one which is much more characteristic of literary language than of ordinary speech. The final type is closely related to this fourth one and is also common in literary language. It consists of a participial adjective or even an infinitive followed by a series of words dependent on it. Since participles and infinitives are non-finite parts of the verb, they cannot act as the predicator of a clause, but they still retain sufficient of their verbal nature to be able to take an object dependent upon them. Hence it is possible to have a noun group like *The dragon, breathing fire and smoke*, in which *dragon* is the head and *breathing fire and smoke* is the qualifier. *Breathing* is a participial adjective from the verb *to breathe*. As such it can take an object, in this case *fire and smoke*, which is what is being 'breathed' by the dragon. The use of participles is common in literary language, partly because they promote brevity in expression through elision of the subject and partly because they may encourage ambiguity because, if the participial adjective is separated from its head, it may be difficult to recognise precisely to which head it refers.

As we noted a moment ago although it is possible to have an unlimited number of modifiers, normally there are not more than three. With qualifiers, on the other hand, not only is it possible to have an unlimited number, but also it is very common to have more than three in some varieties of English. The different types enumerated in the previous paragraph can be mixed. In other words, once the head has been reached it is possible to add information about that head in an incremental way. However, it must be recognised that the accumulation of qualifiers is not without problems. The most pressing one is the decision as to what a particular qualifier refers to, or perhaps it might be better to say whether a head has one or two qualifiers. For example, it is possible to interpret the group *the car in the garage which is old-fashioned* in two ways. The *which is old-fashioned* may refer to *the car* and thus be a second qualifier to that head, or it may refer to *the garage* and thus form part of the single qualifier to the head *car*. Since qualifiers are added incrementally to a head, they may not in speech be organised in the best order and writers may try to exploit this uncertainty. We have to make the best sense of the group we can, and we usually rely on the context or on our own knowledge of what is being reported. In writing, punctuation may help to clarify the meaning, but it is not always a certain guide.

I mentioned earlier that there could be five elements in a noun group and so far I have enumerated only four. The fifth occurs infrequently and is known as a pre-determiner, for it is possible to have certain words in front of a determiner. In a sentence like *All the boys are here*, there is an *all* which precedes *the* and cannot be placed after it. It is mostly words like *all* and *half*, which indicate quantity, that act as pre-determiners.

Because the verb group cannot be extended in the same way as the noun group, it follows that in most forms of literary writing it is the noun group which will carry the bulk of linguistic embellishment because it is the unit of language which can be expanded and adapted most. This nature we may now consider against the examples in Shakespeare's Sonnet 129. The opening sentence has as its first subject *TH'expence of Spirit in a waste of shame*, in which *expence* is the head and *of Spirit in a waste of shame* are two qualifiers which refer to it. But the second qualifier *in a waste of shame* really refers to the whole of the preceding part of the group, *expence of Spirit*. The complement of the first clause in this sentence is *lust in action*, which is formed in the same way as the subject in that it consists of a noun group which has a head and a qualifier. This accentuates the parallelism between the subject and the complement, and suggests that there is a link between *expence of Spirit* and *lust* on the one hand and between *in a waste of shame* and *in action* on the other.

The second clause of this opening sentence has *lust* as its subject, a simple noun group with only a noun as head in it. But the complement is far longer, running as it does for almost six lines (3–8). It is helpful to quote this complement in full before it is subjected to analysis:

> periurd, murdrous, blouddy full of blame,
> Sauage, extreame, rude, cruell, not to trust,
> Inioyd no sooner but dispised straight,
> Past reason hunted, and no sooner had

Past reason hated as a swollowed bayt,
On purpose layd to make the taker mad.

The first two lines of this complement are parallel, for the first
line has three adjectives followed by the phrase *full of blame*,
meaning 'blameworthy', and the second line has four adjectives
followed by the phrase *not to trust*, meaning 'untrustworthy'.
Each line then consists of single-word adjectives followed by
a three-word phrase. The adjectives are usually bisyllabic and
carry the metrical stress for each adjective forms one metrical
foot. The end of each line seems a little more powerful as that
pattern is disrupted. This sequence of adjectives is unusual in
ordinary English because adjectives tend not to follow the noun,
and when they do they are more often separated by *and*. This is
an extreme example of an incremental progression. It is possible
that this list of adjectives is meant to suggest an ascending order
of unpleasantness, though this might be difficult to substantiate.

After these two lines the complement becomes phrasal and
relies now on participial forms. Whereas in the first two lines
there is a sequence of adjectives, in the latter lines contrast and
parallelism are predominant. The third line of the complement
is divided into two elements *Inioyd no sooner* and *but dispised
straight*. Each element consists of a past participle and an adjunct,
and the two are separated by the adversative conjunction *but*. It
seems at first as though the complement is going to continue in
the same vein with rather pat contrasts, for it then goes on
Past reason hunted, which consists of an adjunct and a past
participle. But at this point the neatly balanced contrasts break
down for the second half of the contrast to this adjunct and past
participle embraces the whole of the last two and a half lines of
the complement. Although this is so, the way in which this final
part is arranged makes it have links with what has gone before.
The opening part *and no sooner had* echoes and contrasts with
the phrase *Inioyd no sooner* in the previous line. It also is made
up of an adjunct and a past participle and this order echoes the
order of the first half of the line *Past reason hunted* as well as
that of the following line *Past reason hated*. But the *no sooner
had* is not itself an independent phrase set in contrast with *Past
reason hunted*, since as a whole it forms an adjunct to the head of
the following line. The participles are used to create compression

through ellipsis, for the sense is 'as soon as lust has been satisfied, it is hated immeasurably'. The phrase *Past reason hated* naturally echoes *Past reason hunted* not only in the repetition of the first two words but also in the consonance of the third. This clear marking of the parallelism is necessary because the second part of the contrast is, as we have seen, expanded over two and a half lines, and so readers need to be able to pinpoint precisely what part of that long second element they should focus on. The *hated* is followed by a simile introduced by *as*, the whole of which acts as a kind of adjunct of manner referring to this *hated*. This adjunct consists of a noun phrase which is made up of determiner *a*, modifier *swollowed*, head *bayt* and a long qualifier *On purpose layd to make the taker mad*. The *swollowed* which is itself a participial adjective represents the first time in this sonnet that an adjective or modifier occurs before a noun or head. Since the occurrence of an adjective before a noun is one of the most common orders in English, it may be appreciated from this fact that the organisation and word order of the sonnet are not as ordinary as one might suppose. The qualifier to the head *bayt* is organised with an adjunct *On purpose* referring to the past participle *layd*, which here has a verbal function to enable it to be followed by another non-finite verb, the infinitive *to make*, which with the rest of the line acts as a further adjunct to *layd*.

Some further points need to be raised about this complement. In organisation it is arranged in an ascending order in that it starts with single words, then progresses to short phrases composed of adjunct and participle, and finally arrives at a long two-and-a-half-line element. The complement gets heavier as it progresses, and this movement suggests development. A more difficult problem is whether one should think of it as a single complement, which is how I have referred to it hitherto, or as a whole series of complements. It is clear that the various parts of the complement are closely related and consequently it is natural to think of it as a single complement. If that is the case, then one would have to take *periurd* as the head of the group with all the remaining parts of the complement as qualifiers in apposition to it. Alternatively one could take each element in these lines as a separate complement, though that might seem a little fussy.

The organisation of the second sentence is somewhat different as we saw in the previous chapter. The first four and a half lines of this sentence constitute the object to the verb *knowes*, and this object stands as a mirror image to the complement which concludes the first sentence. This object consists of a noun group, as all objects must, whose head is *this* which is its final word. The *All* has to be understood as a kind of pre-determiner, since pronouns like *this* are not normally able to have modifiers in front of them. The first four lines have to be understood as a kind of qualifier which has been placed in front of the head rather than after it, and this represents a dislocation of normal word order which is acceptable in poetry. The first line starts with *Mad*, which echoes the last word of the preceding complement and so develops what has been already stated there. This opening object then continues:

Mad In pursut and in possession so,
Had, hauing, and in quest to haue extreame,
A blisse in proofe and proud and very wo,
Before a ioy proposd behind a dreame.

Each line forms a complete sense unit, the first and the last being organised on a contrastive basis and the middle two on a three-fold progression. Although the head of this noun group can be said to be *this* in line 13, the preceding four lines do not refer specifically to *this*, which acts rather as a summation than as a point of reference. For the *Mad* of line 9 refers to lust or, by implication, to the person who succumbs to lust rather than directly to the *this* of line 13. This is one reason which enables the qualifier to come before the head and it helps to explain how these four lines tie in with the previous lines of the sonnet, for the reference of the complement at the end of the previous sentence is to lust.

In the first line of this sentence *pursut* and *possession* are set in contrast and both depend upon *Mad*. But the meaning of *Mad* here is perhaps slightly different from that of the previous line, for here the sense seems to mean something like 'excessive, outrageous', whereas before it implies perhaps something more depraved. The sense of 'excessive' ties up with *extreame* in the next line, though that is better understood as an adverb rather than as an adjective, and as an adverb it applies to *had, hauing and in quest to haue*. This line has a three-unit structure which reverses the order of the previous one. In the first line *pursuit* is followed by possession, but in the second there is a sequence of post-possession, i.e. *had*, possession, i.e. *hauing*, and pursuit, i.e. *in quest to haue*. Here we have three non-finite forms of the verb, namely the past participle, the present participle, and the infinitive. Each is adjectival and refers to lust in practice. The next line is somewhat different, because there is a noun *blisse* which is the first time a noun has been used in apposition to a head in this object or in the complement of the previous sentence. Furthermore it is in a series of three, one of which is certainly an adjective, *proud*, and the other was used either as noun or adjective, *wo*. The fact that it is modified by the intensifier *very* suggests that in this line *wo* should be understood as an adjective in the sense 'painful, tormenting'. This indicates that the line may have both progression and contrast, the progression going from joy through pride and pain, and the contrast putting joy and pain in opposition to each other. The final line also uses nouns in apposition, in this case *ioy* and *dreame*. These two words seem to be set in contrast because of the *Before* 'in advance' and *behind* 'afterwards', and so *dreame* suggests something unreal or insubstantial. Lust is not a pleasure which lasts, but which passes into something unreal. One cannot cling on to it for more than a second, it is implied. In this line the use of the determiner *a* before *a ioy* and *a dreame* increases the link with *A blisse* in the previous line. In organisation these four lines have various interconnecting links which help to weld them together.

The rest of the sonnet needs little comment as regards the noun groups. The two subjects of the two clauses in this sentence, *the world* and *none*, are simple groups which need no further discussion. The final line of the sonnet forms the object of the verb *knowes* and so it has to be accepted as a noun group. But this group is a non-finite clause containing the non-finite verb *To shun* and an object *the heauen that leads men to this hell* dependent upon it. This type of non-finite clause object is not very common, though it is quite acceptable. The object of *shun* is a noun group with determiner, head and qualifier, though the qualifier is itself a clause with its own SPOA order.

Our analysis shows that noun groups, which are normally what occupy the subject, object and complement elements in a clause, can be expanded through many lines, and if this poem is anything to go by forms one of the main rhetorical devices available to poets in their attempt to create a more poetic style. In both the final complement of the first sentence and the opening object of the second it is difficult to decide whether all the units of language go to make up a single clause element or whether they should be regarded as parallel examples of the same element. Does the second sentence open with four objects or are the four units part of a single object which are placed in some form of apposition to one another? In ordinary language it is more usual to make the grammatical link between the various parts of a noun group clear; but in poetry this is less true. This is because poets often produce a series of images in a cohesive chain which are clearly to be understood as part of the same general image, but which may not be linked to one another in any apparent grammatical way.

It is not only poets who behave in this way, for especially among earlier writers of prose a similar organisation and elaboration of the noun group can be found. Consider, for example, the opening of the Epistle Dedicatory in Swift's *A Tale of a Tub*:

I HERE present Your Highness with the fruits of a very few leisure hours, stolen from the short intervals of a world of business and of an employment quite alien from such amusements as this; the poor production of that refuse of time, which has lain heavy upon my hands during a long prorogation of parliament, a great dearth of foreign news, and a tedious fit of rainy weather; for which and other reasons, it cannot choose extremely to deserve such a patronage as that of Your Highness, whose numberless virtues, in so few years, make the world look upon you as the future example of all princes; for although Your Highness is hardly got clear of infancy, yet has the universal learned world already resolved upon appealing to your future dictates with the lowest and most resigned submission; fate having decreed you sole arbiter of the productions of human wit, in this polite and most accomplished age.

This long passage is punctuated as a single sentence and probably has to be interpreted as such. If so it could be analysed in this way. The subject is *I*; *here* is an adjunct; the predicator is *present with*, for this form is used when the direct object follows the indirect object; and there are two objects. The first object which is indirect is *Your Highness*, and the second which is direct is everything from *the fruits* until the end of the sentence. The direct object is a noun group which consists of a determiner *the*, head *fruits*, and a series of qualifiers. After *fruits* there is a normal qualifier consisting of a prepositional phrase which extends from *of a very* till the first semi-colon, since *stolen* expands upon *hours* and is dependent upon it. The first semi-colon indicates the boundary of the first qualifier. After it there is a second qualifier which goes from the first to the second semi-colon. This qualifier is in apposition to the head *fruits*, and indeed is formed in much the same way as the first part of the noun group, since it consists of a determiner *the*, modifier *poor*, head *production*, and a qualifier which consists of an elaborate prepositional phrase. The qualifiers in these two noun groups have much in common; they have similar structures and they both expand on the poverty of a literary offering which has been put together in the time that has been snatched from other, weightier occupation.

The analysis of this object noun group has so far been relatively straightforward since there are two parallel structures, one of which is in apposition to the other. At this point difficulties begin to appear and the analysis becomes more complicated. This is because in earlier periods it was much more common to provide a series of linguistic units within a loose grammatical framework. It seems likely that what follows is part of the noun group, but it is difficult to be certain because of this uncertain grammatical structure. The series of semi-colons and the introduction of *for which and other reasons* at the head of the next unit suggests that Swift is signalling a cohesive series of qualifiers, even though this unit of language has clause rather than group structure with a subject *it* and predicator *cannot choose*. This clause appears to be related causally to what has gone before, and the subject *it* appears to refer back to *poor production* of the preceding qualifier. The same problem applies to the next unit which follows, though that consists of two clauses. One, *although Your Highness is hardly got clear of infancy* is an adjunct which is subordinate to the other which has *the universal learned world* as subject and *has resolved* as predicator. But this clause is introduced at the beginning by *for* which is a subordinating conjunction and indicates that the clause as a whole is subordinated to something which has already preceded. It would appear as though this clause is indeed to be regarded as subordinate to the immediately preceding clause, which would make it an adjunct to the predicator *cannot choose* of the earlier qualifier. However, this uncertainty as to the precise grammatical organisation is not untypical of lengthy noun groups, especially those from earlier periods of English. The same may be said to apply to the final unit of the sentence commencing *fate having decreed*. This is an absolute participial construction, in which *fate* acts as the subject of the participle *having decreed*; but since participles are not finite parts of the verb they cannot act as predicator. Hence this unit could not interpreted as an independent clause; as a non-finite clause, it is part of the qualifier in the original noun group acting as the object of *present with*. This kind of participial construction often has a causal sense, which seems appropriate here, for the meaning must be 'because fate has decreed'. As an expression of causality, it is best to interpret the unit as an adjunct, which like the preceding adjunct is probably dependent upon the *cannot choose* of an earlier qualifier. Hence there is some reason to suggest that the last three units of this sentence, that is from *from which* onwards, can be interpreted best as a single clause which acts as a qualifier in the noun group starting *the fruits*. The first two units act as noun groups in apposition which have many parallels between them; and the last three units which also contain many links among them act as a cumulative clause which is a further qualifier.

There may be other ways in which this rather elaborate sentence in *A Tale of a Tub* could be interpreted, but the one outlined in the preceding paragraph seems the most satisfactory. Taken with the analysis of Sonnet 129, it illustrates how the qualifier of a noun group can be expanded almost indefinitely. It is hardly surprising that, as part of this expansion, the grammatical links in the qualifier should become tenuous.

Because subjects, objects and complements are normally realised by noun groups, it is understandable that the noun group figures frequently in the patterned structure of many literary texts. The noun group consists of the elements determiner, modifier, head and qualifier, and it is very common for one noun group to have an identical pattern with another, and this immediately creates balance or parallelism in the text. Hence one subject may balance another, or a subject may be set against the object or complement. This type of parallelism can be illustrated very easily with examples from the passage in *A Tale of a Tub*. The last two units in that long qualifier end like this, and I have put them under one another to make the similar structure clear:

with the lowest and most resigned submission
in this polite and most accomplished age.

Each of these phrases starts with a preposition. This is followed by two modifiers linked together by *and*: the second modifier is in each case preceded by the intensifier *most*. The phrase ends with a noun acting as its head. Earlier in this large qualifier there is a series of three noun phrases, which all have a similar structure:

a long prorogation of parliament
a great dearth of foreign news
a tedious fit of rainy weather.

Each of these starts with the determiner *a*, followed by a modifier and a single head. The head is in turn followed by a qualifier which is in each case a prepositional phrase. The only difference among these prepositional phrases is that the last two contain modifiers, but the first does not. But from the point of view of phrasal weight, the word *parliament* is sufficiently long and heavy to stand by itself against the other two. This structure which terminates the second qualifier is in fact echoed at the end of the third unit in the qualifier:

the future example of all princes.

This has *the* rather than *a* as its determiner, but it has a modifier, single head, and a qualifier which is made up of a prepositional phrase which contains in its turn a single modifier and head. The similarity in structure of these noun phrases is significant, because they provide one of the means by which the long qualifier is made to cohere together as a single unit and because they also provide some of the rhythmical patterning. In poetry it is possible for a noun group or phrase to occupy half of a line of verse (either before or after the caesura), and this is one of the means used by poets to achieve metrical harmony. It is not difficult to find examples of this in Sonnet 129. Expressions like *Mad In pursut* and *a swollowed bayt* fall easily into a half-line of verse. It is a simple extension of this to allow a noun group to occupy a complete line as Shakespeare does in the opening of the sonnet: *TH'expence of Spirit in a waste of shame.* Here the caesura falls naturally after the head so that the qualifier occupies the second half of the line.

The noun group is one of the most important building blocks available to the writer, and an analysis of the noun groups in any piece of literature will quickly reveal how the author has approached the task of composition. Inevitably there are writers who wish to avoid too much reliance upon the noun group because this writing may seem too stereotyped or literary. Such writers will tend to go in for much shorter noun groups and will often try to avoid using too many modifiers which have often been associated with a poetic diction, as in the eighteenth century. A writer who refuses to develop noun groups will be forced to use shorter sentences and may well appear to write in a style which is simpler and more colloquial. It may also mean that greater emphasis is thrown on other parts of the sentence such as the predicator, and that is something to which we shall turn in the next chapter.

3   Group Structure: The Other Groups

Although the noun group is the most important group in a sentence, we should not underestimate the significance of the verb group and the adverb or prepositional groups which realise the functions of predicator and adjunct respectively. That the noun group carries more weight in sentence structure can be readily appreciated from the stress pattern of poetry. It is difficult to imagine a noun acting as the head of a noun group which does not carry stress, but this need not apply to the head of a verb group. In Shakespeare's Sonnet 129, for example, the verbs in the first sentence do not carry stress:

> Is lust in action, and till action, lust
> Is periurd, murdrous, blouddy full of blame.

In both cases *is* is unstressed. Of course, many predicators will carry stress, but the frequency with which this does not happen is some indication that verbs may be less significant in a sentence than nouns. The same applies to adjuncts which are also often unstressed in poetry. Because of the structure of English sentences, the predicator is regularly sandwiched between the noun group acting as subject and that acting as object or complement. The more that either of these noun groups is expanded, the more the verb group is likely to be reduced in importance. It is only when the accompanying noun groups are reduced in weight, perhaps by becoming no more than a pronoun, or when the number of predicators is increased through various strategies that the verb group is likely to achieve a predominant role in a sentence. Caesar's famous boast *veni, vidi, vici*, when translated into English, *I came, I saw, I conquered*, still retains more emphasis on the predicators than on the subjects, all of which are identical and are pronouns. It is the verbs in that sentence which are important, but they are so because the subjects have lost some of their importance and there are no other sentence elements.

Each verb group consists of three elements, the auxiliary, the head, and the extension. As with the noun group, the head is the only element which is compulsory, and when it occurs by itself it is always realised by a finite part of a verb. Indeed, the verb group consists much more often of just the head than is true of the noun group. The auxiliary is composed of a limited number of verbs which qualify the meaning of the lexical verb which is the head of the group. These auxiliary verbs are either modals like *may* or *shall*, or the verbs *do, have* and *be* which can also act as the head of a verb group. In *He did come yesterday*, the verb group acting as predicator is *did come*; and that consists of the auxiliary *did* and the head *come*. When there is an auxiliary in the verb group, the head has a participial or infinitive form. In *did come*, the *come* is the base or infinitive form. It is unusual to have more than two or three auxiliaries in any verb group, and the norm is a single auxiliary. Although it is possible to think of verb groups with up to five auxiliaries, such forms are rare. The extension normally consists either of a single prepositional adverb or of a phrase which together with the head forms an idiomatic expression different in meaning from that of the head. *To sit up* has a different meaning from *to sit*, and *kick* in *kick the bucket* is rather different from its use by itself. But extensions do not occur frequently and cannot be expanded since they fall into set idiomatic expressions. This means that there is a definite limit to the potential elaboration of a verb group, for both the auxiliary and the extension are circumscribed as to length. Indeed, it might be said that whereas a noun group carries more weight the more it is extended, the reverse is true of the verb group. It is those verb groups which consist only of the head which are often the most effective. They are also the most frequent, especially in poetry. All the predicators in Sonnet 129 are verb groups which consist of the head alone. In the first sentence there are only two verb groups, both of which consist of *Is*. There are also participial forms of the verb in this sentence, but they do not form verb groups. In the second sentence there are two examples of *knowes*, both in line 13, which form the predicators of the two clauses. However, the second clause contains a final qualifier which is itself a rank-shifted clause with the predicator *leads*. In other words in this sonnet there are five verb groups, each of which consists of a single word and that word is in its turn a form of the third person singular of the present tense. The force of the verbs comes from the similarity of structure which they share, and this contrasts with the variety and elaboration of the noun groups. The simplicity of the verb forms and the use of the third person singular of the present indicative build up the proverbial nature of the utterance by implying that something is permanently so.

As we saw in the first chapter sentences may be either declarative, interrogative or imperative. The last kind differs significantly from the first two in that the imperative verb group has no modal form, makes no distinction in tense and does not employ the passive form. Usually the imperative occurs in the base form of the verb, as in *Come here*. The imperative sentence has no subject and consequently more emphasis is thrown on to the verb group. It is also frequent for imperative sentences to be brief, since they embody commands which need to be short so that they can be remembered and acted upon. It is hardly surprising that imperatives do not occur very frequently in prose and poetry, though they are more common in drama where one character may order another to do something. When imperatives do occur in poetry, for example, they are likely to be very powerful. A good example is the opening of one of Donne's sonnets:

Batter my heart, three-personed God.

Here the use of a verb group as the opening word, a structure readily achievable only with an imperative, creates a forceful shock which attracts the reader's attention immediately.

Declarative and interrogative sentences distinguish modal from non-modal verb groups, are marked for tense, and have to show voice, and these differences need to be discussed further now. Historically English had two tenses, a present and a past tense, and this can still be seen in most verbs since they have a separate form for the past tense, which I will call the preterite. Hence we have a present tense *he comes* and a preterite *he came*. However, other languages such as Latin and French have a much wider range of tenses, and English writers when translating from these languages tried to imitate those tenses. To form such tenses they had to rely on auxiliaries so that the future tense could be expressed as *he shall/will come*. But the modal auxiliaries had already been used in English to express other concepts; *shall*, for example, expressed obligation as in the Ten Commandments. Equally in the past English distinguished between indicative and subjunctive forms of the verb, but the latter gradually died out as the inflexional system became simplified. Auxiliaries like *should* and *would* have been used instead of the subjunctive forms to some extent so that it is possible to have *If he should come* as well as *If he comes*. The influence of Latin is probably significant in this development too. That certainly applies to the formation of the passive in English, since there was no passive in Old English. A passive form gradually developed from Middle English times onwards, but the passive form did not become popular until well after the Renaissance. However, it is much less clear what caused the adoption of the *do* form in English, which grew in popularity at about the same time as the passive. At first its use was stylistic rather than structural, though it has since become more regulated. The historical dimension in the development of these verbs is important because most of these forms with auxiliaries are regarded as somewhat literary and heavy. They are much more characteristic of written as compared with colloquial style, and their use in a literary text creates a tone which may veer towards the pompous though there are naturally particular uses to which they may be put. Because of their length such verb groups may lack the crispness and directness of the simple forms.

Verbs are essential to clauses and are much more closely related to the form and function of a clause than are nouns. The addition of an extension to a verb group alters the meaning of the verb itself, for *to kick off* is quite a different verb from *to kick*. The auxiliary on the other hand does not alter the sense of the verb so much as its form and function. The forms *kick* and *must kick* refer to the same action, but they look at it in different ways. The emphasis of the clause is likely to be affected by the form of the verb. This may be considered in relation to the difference between the active and passive forms of a verb. In the active voice the agent is also the subject of the clause so that in 'The IRA sent arms to Ireland', the subject *the IRA* is also the agent doing the sending. This sentence can be expressed in a passive form as 'Arms were sent to Ireland by the IRA'. The use of the passive automatically puts the agent into an adverbial group 'by the IRA', for it is still the IRA who are sending the arms. In the active sentence the subject and the theme are both the IRA, but in the passive form the subject is not the IRA, but the arms. Indeed, it is quite possible in a passive sentence to eliminate the agent altogether, for this sentence could be expressed simply as 'Arms were sent to Ireland'. This omission of the agent puts even more stress on the subject since it is no longer clear who is doing the sending or how the arms arrive. The tone of the sentence is changed drastically. The way in which the passive can be exploited can be seen from an example in *Mansfield Park*. Although it is not a finite verb, but an infinitive, the principle is the same. It occurs in sentence 1 where 'Miss Maria Ward . . . had the good luck to captivate Sir Thomas Bertram, of Mansfield Park, in the county of Northampton, and to be thereby raised to the rank of a baronet's lady'. Here Maria Ward does something active, i.e. she captivates Sir Thomas, and then she experiences something passively, i.e. she is raised to the rank of a baronet's lady. The way in which she achieves this elevation is not made clear, for the process is concealed within the *thereby*. Presumably through the captivation of the baronet she became a lady, but the process of being raised is not made to seem an explicit part of her own action. She did not captivate Sir Thomas in order to be made a baronet's lady; the use of the passive suggests that this elevation followed naturally and without her having to make any moves in that direction. The occurrence of *had the good luck* may suggest that Maria Ward was not a schemer, and her good fortune was indeed a matter of chance rather than the result of a well-laid plan.

A slightly different example occurs later in the same paragraph. In sentence 3 it is noted that Maria Ward 'had two sisters to be benefited by her elevation'. The sense here differs because the passive form suggests both futurity and obligation. After the marriage of one sister, it is natural to expect her other sisters to profit from that marriage in the future. But it is not only natural, there is almost an obligation on the sister and her husband to make sure that the two other girls do indeed benefit from her own good fortune. The benefit to accrue is understood to be both financial and social, though in neither case is the expectation fully realised. A third example occurs in sentence 5 where Miss Ward 'found herself obliged to be attached to the Rev. Mr Norris'. She does not apparently do anything so active as to marry Mr Norris, because that would seem to be both purposeful and deliberate. The way in which she found herself obliged to be attached to him almost suggests that this occurred without her will, as though others had made her do it. In all these cases the action is distanced from the agent, which remains in some cases rather insubstantial and certainly unexplained. The recipient of the action appears not to have planned what took place and is made to seem as though she acquiesced in it rather than welcomed it. The role of these women is that of those to whom things happen rather than that of those who make things happen. They are at the whim of others.

Verbs indicate an action or a state, referred to respectively as dynamic and stative. The latter are those like the verb *to be* which indicate a state which does not change or at least appears not to. In Sonnet 129, as we have seen, all the main verbs are stative and this is why the poem appears to be descriptive and proverbial in tone, because it describes what is permanently true rather than something which is changing. Dynamic verbs describe an action which implies a change of state or movement, and actions can be viewed from different points of view. Nouns which refer to a concrete object such as a wall have relatively clear-cut limits as to their description. Walls may be of different materials, width and height, but it is clear enough where a wall begins and ends. This is much less true of a verb. If we say that 'The ship entered the harbour', the verb can refer to various stages in the ship's movement from out at sea right up to the time it ties up at the quay. The ship will pass from the sea through the entrance in the sea wall, sail through the main harbour and ultimately manoeuvre to tie up at a quay. All of this movement or only some of it may be referred to as *to enter* the harbour. Similarly, if one wrote 'The woman stopped the car', the action implied is all the time from applying the brakes until the car stops. Actions can also be repeated in several different ways. An action can be repeated randomly or it can be repeated only whenever another action has happened. In the last line of Sonnet 129 'To shun the heauen that leads men to this hell', the verb *leads* indicated a habitual action which operates on all those who enter that particular heaven.

Verbs and the actions they represent may be viewed in different ways, and usually those differences are expressed through the auxiliaries which occur as part of the verb group, though they may also be indicated through adverbs, particularly adverbs of manner. Modal auxiliaries are important in this respect. Modals have become more frequent in English as the use of the subjunctive has declined. Some writers use auxiliaries simply to make their verb groups longer, and this is especially true today of some types of bureaucratic language. It is probably true that the use of many different verb types is more characteristic of the novel than it is of poetry. Poems tend to use simple tenses, as is true of narrative sequences in a novel. But novels which rely on psychological investigation often make use of auxiliaries to indicate the range of possible activity represented by the verbs. In particular different verbs may be used to suggest either the gap between wish and reality or the distinction between different types of behaviour. Hardy in *Jude the Obscure* can write:

> Somebody might have come along that way who would have asked him his trouble, and might have cheered him by saying that his notions were further advanced than those of his grammarian. But nobody did come, because nobody does.
>
> (Bk 1, ch. 4)

In this short passage the ideas which Jude has are represented by heavy verb groups: *might have come along, would have asked, might have cheered*. These are set into contrast by the abrupt and shorter groups: *did come, does*. Reality is short and painful, whereas dreams seem longer and more fanciful through the choice of verb tenses employed. Even in a passage like this it would have been possible to use less heavy verb groups in the first sentence, such as 'Somebody will come along that way to ask him his trouble and to cheer him'. Hardy has chosen heavy verb groups deliberately, partly because they are parallel with each other and contrast with the short groups, and partly to indicate the wishful thinking which lies behind the ideas.

It is also important to recognise that there is an important difference in tone between transitive and intransitive verbs. Transitive verbs have an object and so indicate an action which has an effect upon someone or something other than the subject. Transitive verbs seem consequently to be more decisive and planned in their operation. Thus if you say 'The boy killed the man', the action of killing which affected the man seems to be both deliberate and planned, although this need not in fact be so in all cases. If, however, one uses an intransitive verb, which has no object, the action may seem to have no particular purpose or intention. Thus if one says 'The man died', there is no object because the verb is intransitive. Equally the fact that the man died is one of those actions for which no cause is implied and certainly no sense of deliberateness or intention is suggested. In some ways intransitives resemble passives because the action may have no agent expressed. It may also shift the point of view of the action. If one contrasts 'She opened the door' with 'The door opened', the point of view in the first is focused on the 'She' who is opening the door. The action of opening the door is less important than who is carrying out the opening. In the second the agent is not expressed and the action is apparently seen from the point of view of people in the room where the door is being opened. Who is opening the door is less significant than the fact that the door is opening. In a well-known essay Halliday has shown how William Golding exploits this type of distinction in *The Inheritors*.[1] The novel depicts the coming of *homo sapiens* as seen from the view of the existing people of a Neanderthal type. The two sets of people use language in a different way in that the original people use verbs which are either stative or intransitive so that many of the actions seem to have no agent performing them. They simply happen. The verbs suggest that these people have not imposed themselves on their environment and cannot direct their activity in a meaningful way. They experience events rather than cause them. The new people, on the other hand, use many transitive verbs in a goal-directed way as though they are causing the events which take place. Their greater mental and physical control is expressed through the verb forms in a significant way. We are not so much told that one set of people is superior to the other, we see that they are so through the linguistic forms associated with each one.

It is important not only to see what type of verb is employed by an author, but also to consider what tense may be used. Within the present tense, for example, it is possible to use either the simple present, the continuous present, or the *do* form. There are differences in emphasis among these forms. The continuous present is used for something which depicts an immediate activity which is happening at the time and may not continue, whereas the simple present indicates something which is true at the time and may continue to be so indefinitely. *She is living in Sheffield* is more temporary than *She lives in Sheffield*, for in the latter case Sheffield would be understood to be her permanent home. The continuous present has grown in popularity recently because it appears to provide more immediacy to what is being said; it is common in spoken language. Naturally in literature, which often refers to events in the past or to matters which are relevant for all time rather than just for the moment, the continuous present is found less often. In dialogue in novels one might expect to find it because it will help to provide that feeling of colloquial immediacy which some novelists strive after. The *do* form, on the other hand, is today restricted to certain types of sentences such as the negative and the interrogative or to promote emphasis. In the past it was used rather more freely and it is sometimes difficult to detect any difference between forms with and without *do*. Often the *do* form gives the style of the passage in which it occurs a more elevated tone partly because it is longer and partly because it is the less common form.

Verbs, as already noted, indicate action and actions occur in a sequence, if they are not thought to occur simultaneously. Caesar's boast 'I came, I saw, I conquered' contains three verbs which represent three actions which happen one after the other in the order in which they occur in his statement. To change the order of the verbs in his statement would be either to create nonsense or to order the actions in a new sequence. This sequential nature of verbs does not apply to noun groups. The modifiers of a noun group may have a preferred order, but that has nothing to do with sequencing, if only because most noun groups are descriptive in a concrete sense rather than indicative of activity. If there is no preferred order of modifiers, there can be no difference in sense with changes to their order: 'the distinctive, large fireplace' is no different from 'the large, distinctive fireplace'. The same applies to nouns which are co-ordinate heads of a noun group. 'The chairs and tables were stacked up neatly' is the same as 'The tables and chairs were stacked up neatly'. Because verbs indicate activity, their order is important and should be studied. Earlier in the chapter I quoted the opening words of a Donne sonnet, and now it is appropriate to quote a somewhat lengthier passage:

Batter my heart, three-personed God, for you
As yet but knock, breathe, shine, and seek to mend;
That I may rise and stand, o'erthrow me and bend
Your force to break, blow, burn, and make me new.

In these lines there is a parallelism between *knock, breathe, shine, and seek to mend* in line 2 and *break, blow, burn, and make me new* in line 4. Our natural inclination is also to think of these activities as taking place in a set order. The knocking precedes the breathing, which in turn precedes the shining and that leads to the heart being mended. We understand the verbs and their implications from the order in which they occur. In line 4 it is necessary to break a heart before it can be burned and hence recreated as new. In the first two lines we understand a series of activities which merely lead to something being mended, whereas in the last two a different series of activities leads to the heart being completely remade. Each activity is part of a patterned series which must proceed in the set order to produce the desired result. It would be impossible to burn something before breaking it to make it new.

Not all the verbs in this Donne passage are finite verbs, but even non-finite verbs can carry on the implication of actions in a sequence. In Sonnet 129 it is clear that 'Inioyd no sooner but dispised straight' represents two actions which follow each other; the enjoyment comes before the despising. In this case the adjuncts and the conjunction *but* make clear that these non-finite verbs still have a sense of activity. The same applies to the infinitives in the opening sentence of *Mansfield Park*, where the *to captivate* indicates an action which precedes the *to be raised*. However, in Sonnet 129 there is a line in which the non-finite verbs do not occur in the order one would expect, and that is line 10: 'Had, hauing, and in quest to haue extreame'. One would expect lust to occur in the three stages: the desire to possess (*in quest to haue*), the possession (*hauing*), and the aftermath of that possession (*had*). Their reversal is unusual and underlines the *extreame* nature of these actions. They appear to be contrary to nature because their order is also unnatural. Some features of the preceding discussion can be illustrated by looking at a short passage from *Henry Esmond*:

She stretched out her hand – indeed when was it that that hand would not stretch out to do an act of kindness, or to protect grief and ill-fortune? 'And this is our kinsman,' she said; 'and what is your name, kinsman?'

'My name is Henry Esmond,' said the lad, looking up at her in a sort of delight and wonder, for she had come upon him as a *Dea certè*, and appeared the most charming object he had ever looked on. Her gold hair was shining in the gold of the sun; her complexion was of a dazzling bloom; her lips smiling, and her eyes beaming with a kindness which made Harry Esmond's heart to beat with surprise.

(Ch. 1)

The first verb *stretched out* is in the preterite, as is common in narration in novels. The present is used only when the author wishes to create more immediacy and emphasis. The *would not stretch out* has the auxiliary *would*, which here suggests the subjunctive and hence appears to be hypothetical. It is not as definitive in its implication as *did* would be. The verb form is unusual in that *stretch out* is normally transitive, but is here intransitive. It almost implied that the hand would stretch out of its own accord when it encountered any misfortune; the action is seen as virtually involuntary. The goodness of the lady is such that she could not prevent her hand from stretching out whenever she saw distress. The distinction between the transitive and intransitive forms is reinforced because the same verb is used in each clause. After a series of stative verbs, we have in the second paragraph a variety of different tenses. In addition there are several participial forms in *-ing* used as modifiers and as heads of verbal groups. These forms echo one another, but also introduce an element of immediacy as though they reflect the boy's own visual response. *Her gold hair was shining* reflects both his attitude and his response to her more clearly than *Her gold hair shone* would do, for that would seem little more than straightforward description. There is also a sense of parallelism between *looking up* and *looked on*. The latter verb suggests a sense of wonder and intensity which *seen* would not have. The two extensions to each verb, *up* and *on*, help to underline the boyish nature of the activity expressed. The difference between *had come upon him* and *appeared* is that the former indicates a single action, whereas the latter suggests something which is a continuing feature. Although these few comments do not exhaust all that might be said about the verb forms, they perhaps provide a model for what verbs can tell us and how they mould our response to the text.

Adjuncts may be expressed through adverb or prepositional groups, which may contain one or more words, or through clauses. The variety is shown in the following sentences where the adjunct is italicised:

1 *Yesterday* she went to London.
2 *In the morning* she went to London.
3 *When she received the message*, she went to London.

In each sentence the adjunct represents an adverbial of time, though there are many other meanings which can be expressed by adjuncts as we shall see. Perhaps it needs first to be remembered that the adjunct is the least essential sentence element. Almost all sentences have a subject and a predicator, and the majority also require an object or complement. The adjunct is an optional element, and because it is optional its position in the sentence is freer. In each of the sentences above the adjunct could have been placed as the final element:

1a She went to London *yesterday*.
2a She went to London *in the morning*.
3a She went to London *when she received the message*.

Changing the position of the adjunct does have some bearing on the emphasis it receives, but that emphasis will not be as strong as is the case when the subject is put in a different position from the one expected.

Because the adjunct is optional there is usually another way in which a sentence containing one can be written, particularly with clausal adjuncts. Sentence 3 could readily appear as two sentences, and even sentence 2 could, though perhaps less naturally, be rewritten:

2b It was morning. She went to London.
3b She received the message. She went to London.

The meaning of 2b and 3b are not identical with those of 2 and 3, though most readers will probably assume they are. It is, therefore, important when examining a text to see how many adjuncts are introduced into each sentence. A plain style will have fewer adjuncts than an elaborate one, because adjuncts lead to subordination and introduce qualification. Most adjuncts qualify the predicator; they introduce qualifications as to how, when or where an action took place. The action does not stand on its own, but it is hedged round with additional features. The action represented by the verb may consequently appear less stark and vivid. This is particularly true if more than one adjunct is included, because the emphasis of the sentence shifts towards the adjuncts, depending on their number. To say *She went to London* puts the focus on the action of going. But to say *She went to London reluctantly* results in the emphasis shifting away from the action of going to the way in which the journey was performed. This would be even more marked if the sentence became *She went to London reluctantly and by a circuitous route*, for the focus is now less on the travelling and more on the desire not to arrive – and these aspects are indicated through the adjuncts. Naturally the lexical choice of verb and adverbial may influence the amount of emphasis each sentence element has, and other factors such as rhyme in poetry may operate. In Sonnet 129 the final line finishes *that leads men to this hell*, in which *to this hell* is an adjunct of place. In the adjunct not only is *hell* the last word of the sonnet, but also it rhymes with *well* and stands in contrast to *heauen*. It carries the main emphasis in the line, and the adjunct has been pushed into much greater prominence than either the subject which is the relatively innocuous *that* or the predicator *leads*. Even the object *men* is so general that it lacks much force and impact. The adjunct can be an important part, perhaps the most important part, of a sentence, but its weight must be balanced against the other elements.

Adjuncts can form part of the balance within a sentence or its groups, as applies in Sonnet 129 in which lines 5–8 have a succession of adjuncts which contrast with one another:

Inioyd *no sooner* but dispised *straight*,
Past reason hunted, and *no sooner* had

> *Past reason* hated as a swollowed bayt,
> *On purpose* layd to make the taker mad.

Here two of the adjuncts are repeated exactly, and most consist of two words which have the same make-up in that the first is an unstressed monosyllable and the second a bisyllable with the stress on the first syllable. This type of parallelism and contrast is more likely to be found within the compressed language of poetry than in drama or prose, though this possibility should never be overlooked even in those kinds of writing. In *Mansfield Park* there are not many adjuncts in the opening paragraph, and most that are found are concerned with time.

Of the many types of adjunct those of time are perhaps the ones most often remarked on. In *Mansfield Park* the novel opens with an adjunct of time *About thirty years ago*, which is echoed in sentence 5 by *at the end of half a dozen years*. There are other types of adjunct and the differences need to be noted. Adjuncts of time and place are often concrete and factual; they do not necessarily contribute much to the tone of the passage. Adjuncts of manner and those which are sometimes known as emphasisers and amplifiers are much more significant for establishing tone and authorial voice. In *Mansfield Park* there are several which are worth noting. In sentence 4 we find 'But there certainly are not so many men . . . ', which could just as easily have appeared as 'But there are not so many men . . . '. This *certainly* suggests an authorial intrusion which not only underlines the sentential statement, but also colours it by implying what a misfortune it is. Sentence 6 begins 'Miss Ward's match, indeed, when it came to the point, was not contemptible, Sir Thomas being happily able to give his friend . . . '. In this sentence the *indeed* throws emphasis on the sentence and suggests some authorial reservations about how happy this match actually was. Later in the sentence it is said that Sir Thomas was *happily* able to provide his friend with an income. It is not clear how we should interpret this *happily* or from whose point of view. Is it we as readers who are happy with this outcome, the author herself, Sir Thomas or the 'happy' couple who were being married? *Happily* is an adjunct which is appropriate to marriages, though the word could well have ironic overtones depending on which point of view we take. This example underlines one of the strengths of adjuncts of this type: the point of view of the manner, emphasis or amplification may be less than clear so that the reader can select from among various possibilities. The result will influence the tone we assign to any passage. Although it may well be that noun groups form the most important element in a sentence, the contribution which the other groups can make should never be overlooked.

4 Vocabulary

Words are the items of language which most readers focus on immediately because in coming to terms with language words often appear to be the core from which meaning springs. Writers themselves often present their composition as a struggle with words. Words are not, however, quite so easy to deal with as syntax because each word has a particular history and each has to be taken on its own terms. Nevertheless, it is possible to offer some general principles with which to tackle the vocabulary in a piece of literature.

Words in English consist of two groups, grammatical and lexical. Grammatical words provide the syntactic framework of a sentence and help us to understand the interrelationship of the lexical words in a sentence. Although essentially grammatical in function, it is not appropriate to think that these words have no meaning, but they have less referential and associative meaning than lexical words. Generally the grammatical words belong to the closed group of words in English, such as article and preposition, that is their number cannot readily be expanded. It is not easy to introduce a new preposition in English. Lexical words are those which carry the major meaning of a sentence and which are thought by most users of the language to be significant and important. These belong to the open group of words, for their number can be expanded indefinitely. The new words constantly being added to the language belong to classes such as the noun class. In a sentence such as 'The boy hopes to come by car', its syntactic pattern is established through the grammatical words: 'The . . . . . . to . . . by . . . '. The gaps represent the lexical words which provide the meaning, and in this case the lexical words are either nouns or verbs. It is the grammatical words which are omitted in telegrams so that the above sentence might appear in a telegram as BOY HOPES COME CAR. The sender anticipates that the receiver will understand the message from the order in which the lexical words appear. It is also lexical words which appear in newspaper headlines at the expense of grammatical ones so that WAVES SINK SHIP is a typical headline.

It is important to bear the distinction between grammatical and lexical words in mind, because the more compressed a style is the more likely it is to abandon grammatical words. Since poetry, particularly lyric poetry, can seek to convey multiple layers of meaning through few words, there is a tendency in poetry to reduce the number of grammatical words. This means that many lexical words are thrown into juxtaposition and this creates density of meaning. Sometimes this may be done, as in Sonnet 129, by having adjectives in a row as in *Sauage, extreame, rude, cruell*. A line composed of many adjectives can stand in contrast with one with many grammatical words, such as the final line in the sonnet: *To shun the heauen that leads men to this hell.* This last line has an expansiveness not found in the earlier one. In poetry one may also notice that the grammatical words usually fill the unstressed metrical positions, and this is one reason why the last line flows so easily; there is a succession of weak and strong stresses which is almost regular. Where the grammatical words are lacking, there is likely to be a clash of stresses as in *extreame, rude, cruell*; and because of this clash the line will seem to be heavier. Naturally, there may be contrast within the line through the absence or presence of grammatical words. In the two lines

Is periurd, murdrous, blouddy full of blame,
Sauage, extreame, rude, cruell, not to trust,

each line ends with a group consisting of a grammatical and a lexical word: *of blame* and *to trust*. The ending of each line not only sets up an echo with the other, but also contrasts with the heavy row of adjectives in the earlier part of the line. These two lines with many lexical words at the beginning and a single grammatical word near the end contrast with line 11, which is also descriptive, but in which there are many grammatical words: *A blisse in proofe and proud and very wo*. It is important to look at the different types of words because they help to provide much of the rhythm of a poem, and the same applies in principle to a piece of prose, though the divergences there are likely to be less marked.

Words also have significant associations because of their historical development, for English has been a language very receptive to borrowing from other languages. Many borrowed words have become so assimilated that many speakers find it difficult to recognise their foreign origin. Other words have dropped out of the language and are now archaic or obsolete. This presents one of the difficulties in reading a piece of literature from an earlier age. A word which to us now seems perfectly ordinary may at the time of composition have been new and evocative; on the other hand, a word which now seems archaic and hence special may at the time of composition have been perfectly normal and unexceptional. One has only to consider some relatively recent borrowings into English to make this plain. A word like *glasnost* is still associated with the USSR and with the reforms introduced by Mr Gorbachev; it is understood to be a Russian word and would frequently be italicised in English. Yet even this word is being extended to contexts which have nothing to do with the USSR, and it may become a word meaning 'freedom of expression' which is available in any context. Another word borrowed in the present century, *apartheid*, is still used principally with reference to South Africa, but is also readily extended to any form of racial segregation, whether in Africa or not. To most people it now seems a common word which expresses a concept which is needed in the language because segregation occurs in so many societies in so many forms. Consequently the word no longer appears to be foreign to most people; for many younger people the word has been part of their lives since they could think and talk. It would be unusual to find this word italicised in a modern piece of writing, because it has largely lost its foreignness.

Traditionally English vocabulary is divided into Saxon and Latin words, for over the last few hundred years controversy has raged as to whether it is better for an author to rely on one type rather than the other. It is usually claimed that Saxon words are monosyllabic, and consequently have strength and vitality. Latin words, on the other hand, are polysyllabic and have a more learned aura attached to them. Because they are polysyllabic, they exhibit variation within the word of stressed and unstressed syllables, and that makes them more adaptable to poetic metres.

Naturally not all Saxon words are monosyllabic or all Latin ones polysyllabic, but there is considerable truth in the distinction. In this connection it may be helpful to say a few words about the growth of the English vocabulary.

When the Anglo-Saxons came to England from the fifth century onwards they brought with them their branch of the Germanic language. This has provided the basic vocabulary of English, and mos⸱ of the common words we use today are likely to have their origins in this period. As English lost its inflexional system and abandoned many of its unstressed syllables, many of these words ended up as monosyllables. Old English poetry used many compound words, though these have rarely survived beyond the medieval period. Compounding still remains a possible means of enlargement of the vocabulary, but English has gone in more for borrowing from other languages than for creating new compounds from words already in the language. Even in Old English times and increasingly since then, English has been subject to cultural influences from the rest of Europe. The introduction of Christianity brought with it many new words, and the Norman Conquest led to the wholesale import of words of French origin. As the higher ranks of society were filled with people of continental origin, French acquired a prestige higher than that of English. This prestige was accentuated by the introduction of French culture and concepts so that many French words were introduced because of their more elevated literary associations. In the Renaissance with the revival of classical Latin, the prestige previously associated with French was diverted to Latin; and many words borrowed from French into Middle English were given a Latinate spelling so that Middle English *dette* became Modern English *debt* (Latin *debitum*). It became fashionable to include many words of Latin origin in one's writing for Latin words were considered to have greater authority and intellectual appeal. Sometimes Latin and English words exist side by side, as in such pairs as *see/perceive* and *bodily/corporal*. The Latin word will almost invariably have the more elevated feel. Over the course of years the words may have become specialised to some extent so that they occur in restricted contexts, but that does not invalidate the general principle that words of English origin belong to a different register from those of Latin ancestry. Since the Renaissance period many words from other languages have been borrowed into the language, but few of those have achieved the status accorded to words of classical origin.

The penetration of French and Latin words into the language can be gauged by looking at the origin of the words in the first few lines of Sonnet 129. Inevitably the words borrowed from French or Latin are lexical words, and the majority are nouns. In the first four lines the following words come from French, though often with a Latin form: *expence, spirit, waste, action, periurd, blame, sauage, extreame, rude* and *cruell*. Of the other lexical words *shame, lust, murdrous* and *blouddy* are from Old English, and *trust* is from Scandinavian. The words of Old English origin are mostly monosyllabic, though with an ending such as -*y* in some cases. Many, but by no means all, of the French words are bisyllabic and several have a rather more formal air as compared with its Germanic equivalent: *expence* (as compared with *cost*), *spirit* (as compared with *ghost*), and *periurd* (as compared with *forsworn*). However, many words of French origin have become so much part of our vocabulary that we would find it difficult today to think of them as anything other than ordinary words; and this would apply to words like *waste, blame* and *rude*. It is for this reason that some scholars think it might be more reasonable to divide the vocabulary into core words and others. If a word is so common that it is used by the majority of the speakers of the language, whatever its precise origin, it is unhelpful to label it a French word as though that somehow made it more exotic than in fact it is. Core words are likely to be monosyllabic and used regularly by all speakers of the language. They are also likely to be more concrete than the other words which may well be polysyllabic, abstract and intellectual in tone.

In Sonnet 129 it is the nouns and adjectives which carry the greatest lexical load, and the verbs not surprisingly are mostly of Old English origin. All the finite verbs are: *is, knowes* and *leads*. Even most of the non-finite verbs are too: *hunted, had, hated, swollowed, layd, make, had, hauing, to haue, shun*; and *trust* as we have seen is Scandinavian. Only *Inioyed, dispised* and *proposd* are from French. When we turn to *Mansfield Park* the situation is different. Not only are the verbs, both finite and non-finite, more important in the opening paragraph, but also many of them are classical in their origins. Consider *captivate, exclaimed, allowed, benefited, scruple, predict, obliged* and *attached*, which are all of

French or Latin origin. In many cases these verbs are designed to give a more decorous tone to the proceedings. It is more acceptable for a lady to *captivate* a future husband than it would be for her to *trap* him, which would have the overtones of hunting an inferior animal. To *exclaim* about a match is much more genteel than to *cry out* about it. It is noticeable that when the two sisters of Miss Maria Ward are commented on, the verbs lose this tone. Miss Frances, for example, *fared yet worse*. Not only is the statement brief, but also its expression is very straightforward, almost downmarket, in tone. The description of Miss Ward's match perhaps comes half-way between the other two in its choice of verbs. Throughout the paragraph the verbs are supported by many nouns and adjectives of a classical origin: *baronet, comforts, consequences, equitable, elevation, acquaintance, advantage, private, fortune, contemptible, career, conjugal, felicity*. As compared with the words in Sonnet 129, these Latinate words are both longer and less common. They are also somewhat abstract, and so put a genteel veneer over the rather more sordid reality of marrying for money and position.

It has been suggested in the previous paragraphs that authors can contrast one kind of vocabulary with another. In the sonnet we saw that lines with many lexical words could be put into contrast with those with many grammatical words. When that happens, it is likely that a similar contrast between words of Latinate and Anglo-Saxon origin will also be revealed. In the last two lines

> All this the world well knowes yet none knowes well,
> To shun the heauen that leads men to this hell

all the words are of Old English origin and all are monosyllabic, for it seems reasonable to accept that Shakespeare understood *heauen* here as a monosyllable. This apparent simplicity suggests an inevitability which contrasts with the rather heavier description of lust in the earlier part of the sonnet. Though sin may be exotic and refined, damnation is straightforward and inexorable. Similarly with the marriages of Miss Maria and Miss Frances, the one is described in Latinate vocabulary and the other in Saxon words. The one is made to seem more than the union of a man and a woman, whereas the other is no more than that. In both cases this contrast is accentuated by the choice in the vocabulary, and the interplay between words of different origins in English is frequently exploited by authors. One of the more famous examples is Macbeth's

> No; this my hand will rather
> The multitudinous seas incarnadine,
> Making the green one red.
>
> (*Macbeth* II.ii.61–3)

In this example there are two long Latinate words in the second line: *multitudinous* and *incarnadine*. They contrast not only with the monosyllabic *seas* which separates them, but also with the simple Saxon words in the third line. That second contrast is made more compelling in that *incarnadine* means exactly the same as *Making . . . red*. The same idea is expressed in both a highly literary and a simple way. It is important in reading a work of literature to keep a note of the type of vocabulary used so that contrasts and parallelisms may be understood. It may not be necessary to examine the origin of every word, for a sampling technique may well lead to decisions as to which passages might be examined in greater depth.

In the words borrowed from another language one may distinguish, as has been suggested, between those words which entered the language through ordinary social usage and became part of the core vocabulary and those words which were introduced by literary writers and may never have entered the spoken language. Writers have always tried to enrich the vocabulary of English either because they felt English was an impoverished language which needed strengthening or because they wanted to create an individual tone of voice for their own writing. There are four principal ways in which the vocabulary of literary English has been distinguished from that of ordinary speech. They are the cultivation of words which have already become or are on the point of becoming obsolete; the use and invention of compound words; the introduction of foreign words of an exotic or learned nature; and the use of functional shift whereby a word which is normally used in one grammatical function is transferred to a different one. It will be helpful to look at each of these in turn.

The use of vocabulary which is obsolete or nearly so is associated with particular authors and certain types of literature. Although the Church of England has taken steps to modernise the language of its liturgy recently, the language of religion is still one which has archaic features in it. It is in that type of language that one might expect to find *thou* and *thee* instead of *you* as well as verbs which have the present form in *-eth* rather than in *-es* as in *cometh* rather than *comes*. Consequently in religious poetry, hymns and poems which have a particularly elevated moral or philosophical tone one may expect to find some archaic vocabulary and morphology. In Gerard Manley Hopkins's poem *Thou Art Indeed Just, Lord* we find archaic forms like *thou*, *thee*, *thy*, *art*, *wert*, *dost* and *wouldst*. He also uses the interjection *O*. There are few archaic nouns in this poem, but words like *sots*, *thralls* and *brakes* are now rare and mainly poetic. Phrases like *lord of life* are restricted and would not be found outside religious contexts. Some of the words and forms of this character are associated with 'poetic' vocabulary, and they can be useful for poets. For example, *cometh* has two syllables as compared to the one of *comes*, and various contracted forms like *o'er* and *e'en* are monosyllabic as compared with their expanded forms. It is important in looking at words like this to decide whether the writer is using them to create a tone suitable for his subject matter or whether he is using them out of laziness because it is a convenient way of completing the metre of his line.

Some poets, of whom Spenser is the best example, have used archaic vocabulary extensively. In Spenser's poetry many of the words which may be called archaic are in fact words invented or introduced by him. Prefixes in *a-*, *dis-* and *en-* and suffixes in *-ful(l)* and *-y* are particularly characteristic of his writing and occur in such forms as *awarm*, *disloign*, *enmove*, *duefull* and *finny*. Not all these words with such affixes are new to English in Spenser, but many are. They give his style a remoteness and difference from the ordinary language of his day. Many words used by Spenser were adopted by his imitators not only in the years immediately after his death but also in later periods. Such words as *steed*, *damozel*, *puissant*, *verdant* and *guerdon* are today both archaic and poetic; Spenser's use has given them a romantic tinge. Yet in his own time such words were not nearly as unusual as they have since become. Each poet takes over words from his predecessors, and Spenser is no exception to this dictum because he took over many words from Chaucer. Gradually words borrowed in this way become isolated from the stock of common words and become poetic, though it is not always easy to say precisely when this happens. It is easy to accuse Spenser of using too many archaisms because so many of his words appear archaic to us today, but from a historical perspective many of them were still far from obsolete at his time. However, later poets like Keats and Tennyson have borrowed many of the Spenserian words to give their writings a more distinctive veneer. Words like *verdant* when used in the nineteenth century have a more specific archaic flavour than they had in the sixteenth.

Apart perhaps from some poetic words, archaisms are not likely to be found in many poems, particularly more recent ones. They are useful for creating an echo to a previous poem or type of poem, and they can help to establish the tone of a particular piece of literature. Archaisms are most likely to be met with in poetry and least likely in novels where a more prosaic language and ordinary speech are more often aimed at. In our Shakespearian sonnet there is only one word which by Shakespeare's time was beginning to be archaic, and that is *wo* which occurs as an adjective. Today *woe* is used only as a noun, but even that is almost obsolete. In Middle English it was possible to use it as an adjective in the sense 'wretched, miserable', and that sense lingered on into the seventeenth century becoming increasingly archaic and dialectal. Other words like *straight* may seem archaic now, but were still common in Shakespeare's time. There are no archaic words in the opening of *Mansfield Park*. These two examples are not untypical of most pieces of literature except for those trying to create a special effect.

Compounding is a process which many regard as typically poetic for it is the process which produces exotic and unusual words. A compound word is one which consists of two independent words such as *awe-inspiring*, for both *awe* and *inspiring* exist separately. Compounds differ from complex words, which contain one independent word and one affix, usually a suffix, which is not a self-standing word. An example of a complex word is *aweful*, since although *awe* is a free-standing word, *-ful* is not for it can occur only in conjunction with other elements. Because English is a Germanic language, it inherited the typical Germanic way of enlarging the vocabulary by creating compounds. Old English poetry is full of compounds. But as English came to borrow more words from other languages, particularly Latin and

Greek, compounding became a less common feature of standard English. Compounding developed two quite contrary tones. Compounds occur still in colloquial language, because it is not likely that ordinary people in their speech will use Latin words to make their language more colourful. Compounding being a traditional means of enlarging the vocabulary is still used to make it evocative. A word like *gogglebox* for *television* is one which fits into this pattern of creating an evocative colloquial style. On the other hand, compounding was still used by poets as a means of creating a high style, because compounding had been the original poetic means of stylistic enhancement. Compounding also has the virtue for poets that it creates words whose meaning is transparent to users of the language, whereas words borrowed from other languages will be readily understandable only to those people familiar with the language from which the word is borrowed. Thus the word *incarnadine* quoted earlier in the chapter is not one that most English people will understand immediately unless they have some knowledge of Latin. If, however, one were to invent compounds like *red-making* or *all-reddening*, the average speaker of the language would have no problem in understanding what was meant. A further advantage of compounding is that it is possible to promote echoes between words because they use the same word either by itself or as part of a compound. Thus there is no apparent link between *heaven* and *celestial* apart from that of meaning. But there is between *heaven* and *heaven-blue*, *heaven-high* or *heaven-sweet*. If these words occurred in a poem together, they would create a direct link through vocabulary and sound with one another which would not be possible between the words *heaven* and *celestial*. The repetition of a word either by itself or as part of a compound is important for achieving cohesion within language as we shall see in a later chapter.

There are no compounds in the Shakespeare sonnet or in the opening paragraph of *Mansfield Park*. The absence of compounds in a novel is hardly surprising, but their absence in the sonnet is noteworthy since Shakespeare is a writer famed for his use of compounds, many of which are very striking. Their absence should remind us that writers have available many ways of enriching their language, and we should not expect all of them to appear in any piece of writing. In Sonnet 129 where there are strings of adjectives and where parallelism and contrast are important features, the use of compounds might have made certain words too heavy and marked for the context. Naturally some writers exploit compounds more than others; in an earlier period Shakespeare used them extensively, and more recently Dylan Thomas has made great use of them.

The borrowing of foreign words has already been mentioned in this chapter, particularly in reference to French and Latin. English is a world language and as a result of the British Empire the language has been adopted as a first or second language in many parts of the world. It therefore continues to borrow words from languages throughout the world. But one needs to distinguish among the languages which could give words to English on the basis of their cultural and political influence. Words may well be borrowed from any language to provide the necessary background colour for a novel or poem set in the country where the language was spoken. A novel about South Africa may well use words of Afrikaans origin such as *laager* and *veldt* because such words reflect the social and geographical conditions there. They are technical rather than literary. South Africa is not a country with such political weight internationally or with a culture which other countries might wish to emulate. No particular prestige attaches to the words in its language, and there is no impetus to borrow words more generally. Afrikaans as a language will have a restricted impact on the vocabulary of English. In the past Latin and Greek had enormous prestige, and although they are less commonly studied today they still represent the countries which established European culture. The Greek language is associated with the development of philosophy and many other educational and scientific developments; Latin was the language of the Roman Empire and became the language of the Roman Catholic Church, and as such has contributed to all European languages. Even today to know the classics is regarded as a sign of education and sophistication; consequently the use of classical words is promoted. Furthermore, many of the narratives and myths known to most people are, if not religious, classical in origin, and these often appear as thematic motifs in many works of literature and help to underline the classical basis of our own literary culture.

Of modern languages French continues to be the most important culturally since so many cultural influences from the rest of Europe come to us through the medium of French. English schoolchildren almost invariably learn French as their first, and often only, foreign language. France is still held up as a model in so many fields of life, of which literature, cuisine and fashion are merely the better known. Increasingly the recognition that there are only two superpowers, the USA and the USSR, has meant that both are likely to influence the English language. Americans speak English, but have a vocabulary which is both different in many ways and subject to other influences. For English people the USA has become associated with particular cultural activities such as jazz, the pop scene, drugs and American football – to name but a few. Many have had a profound influence on some aspects of English lexis, but as older people often resent that influence words of American usage are met with criticism rather than welcomed. The USA is also associated with the loosening of more formal attitudes to language, and this in turn has meant that Americanisms are more likely to be found in language which is colloquial in style today. The impact of the American language has been most felt in the twentieth century. Russian has still to make much impact despite the importance of the USSR herself. This may be accounted for partly because so few English people know any Russian and partly because there are so few cultural features of Russian life which English people care to imitate. Russian music and ballet are admired, but they have produced no lexical borrowings. The few words that have entered the language have been either technical, associated particularly with space travel, or political, associated with labour camps or the possible liberalisation of the political and economic system. Russian novels and plays have been translated into English since the nineteenth century, but their linguistic influence has been slight. Attitudes to the Russian political system have tended to be so disapproving, particularly as regards the dangers of communist aggression, that linguistic borrowing has been inhibited.

Although all languages are available as potential quarries for words, in practice few of them are exploited to any extent. Only those which carry prestige or whose words might be expected to be familiar to an educated person are likely to be ransacked. Consequently, it is still from the classical languages and from a limited number of modern languages that most English writers borrow. Since today the emphasis in many literary works is on plainness rather than on elaboration, the importation of foreign words is less likely to occur because that might smack of too much ostentation.

Functional shift, however, has been a much greater source of verbal development in more recent literature, though as a technique it has been available since the early modern period. When English was an inflected language, when the role of words as noun or verb was indicated through an inflexional ending, functional shift was difficult if not impossible. As English lost its inflexional endings, it became possible for words to occupy a multiplicity of functions because there was nothing which made a word a noun rather than a verb. There is nothing in the word *run* which marks it out as a noun, verb or adjective; its role is decided by the position it occupies in the sentence. This variation is possible only for those words which belong to the open classes: nouns, verbs, adjectives and adverbs. The grammatical words cannot have their function changed.

The most common form of functional shift is to change a noun into an adjective or a verb, a shift which is common in ordinary language as well as in literary language. So common have some of these changes become that speakers of the language no longer think of them as exceptional. The verb *scruple* in *Mansfield Park* has been shifted from the noun *a scruple*, but this happened in the seventeenth century and the verb has been accepted as quite natural ever since. Indeed, in literature of the past many examples of functional shift which were new when they first appeared are now so common as to excite no interest. Consequently it is in more modern literature that the most striking examples are found, though there are still some in Shakespeare which are breath-taking in their inventiveness such as *braine* 'to think about' and *knee* 'to kneel'. Writers with a compact style are likely to use functional shift because it is through the profusion of lexical words that compactness is created. When, as is not uncommon in some modern writing, punctuation is limited or even non-existent, it may be difficult to decide what function a particular word has. When Dylan Thomas in 'A Refusal to Mourn the Death, by Fire, of a Child in London' has 'Bird beast and flower / Fathering', it is difficult to decide whether *bird*, *beast* and *flower* should be regarded as nouns shifted to function as adjectives referring to *fathering* or treated as nouns parallel to it. Without a comma between *bird* and *beast*, one is uncertain whether one should take those two items as a single compound *bird-beast* or as two separate words *bird* and *beast*. The absence of inflexional endings in English enables authors to throw words together in this way to create multiple layers of meaning in their text so that the reader in teasing out the meaning goes through various possibilities. The reader has to decide whether this type of lexical organisation is nothing more than a kind of complexity for its own sake or whether it adds significantly to the levels of meaning in the poem, for it is a feature of poetry much more than of the novel or drama.

Writers develop their vocabulary not only by introducing new words, but also by using words in senses or contexts which are new. Many words in normal English are restricted to particular spheres and as a consequence occur with other words within that same field of meaning. By putting a word into a different context writers can open up a new and suggestive area of meaning for their readers. Often this forms the basis of literary metaphor, though metaphor can also be created by other means such as functional shift. In the opening line of Sonnet 129 Shakespeare refers to *TH'expence of Spirit in a waste of shame*. *Expense* has the sense of spending or using up something, usually of a material or physical nature, for to use something up suggests that it is of a finite amount which without proper care can be entirely exhausted. It can also be applied to abstracts, but this is less common. Because of links with *expenditure* and *expensive*, *expence* has a monetary implication as though it is a matter of buying and selling. *Spirit* being abstract is not usually associated with monetary values of cost and benefit, nor is it something which can be used up like food or material necessities. Its link with expense suggests that in this context it is something valuable because it costs money and that consequently it should not be squandered away thoughtlessly. It has a rather more physical and material feel than usual. *Waste* can have two major senses in this period, one 'desert, wasteland' and the other 'unnecessary loss or consumption'. Both senses may be implied here. The latter sense links up with *expence*, since it is suggested the spirit is used up entirely in a foolish and unnecessary manner. What should have been conserved is destroyed. Its destruction leads to barrenness, which is the other sense of *waste*. *Shame* is an abstract word indicating the emotion aroused by wrong or anti-social behaviour. Such emotion could well lead to a sense of desolation and barrenness, as implied through *waste*. Hence it is suggested both that the spirit may have been used up through wastefulness and that this exhaustion led to an emotion of emptiness and isolation. As expense and waste are usually linked with words of a physical or material sense, it gives the abstract words in the first line a more substantial feel to them and leads one to assume that *lust* in the next line has a physical expression, even though no physical attribute is mentioned.

It is important to bear in mind that words have two types of meaning, a denotative and a connotative meaning. The denotative meaning is the meaning one might find in a dictionary, whereas the connotative meaning is the associations which attach to the word arising partly through the contexts in which it occurs and the other words with which it is normally found. For example, *spirit* is the soul or animating life-force of sentient beings and is associated with the divine life-force. As such it is something which is good, valuable and worth preserving. It is often thought of as being indestructible, for it stands in contrast to the body which is both weak and temporary. Human beings are themselves the battleground between the body, which has physical needs and desires which seek to be satisfied, and the soul or spirit, which is the nobler part of the person because it is that which is more closely related to the divine. Humankind's spirit is indestructible in the sense that it is not mortal and human, but it may be corrupted and destroyed through the body. The connotative senses of *spirit* might be said to be all good, but those of *expence*, *waste* and *shame* are unfavourable. The first two are so because they indicate the exhaustion of that which could and should have been preserved; the last one because *shame* is linked with behaviour which fails to come up to the social norm.

Lust is a word which has gone down in the world. Originally it meant 'pleasure' and had no connotation of disapproval. Gradually it became linked with physical, particularly sexual, pleasure, and as sexual pleasure was attacked in most forms of Christian teaching, *lust* lost its innocent associations and became little more than 'the gratification of sexual inclinations without concern for the other party', hence *lust* comes to be seen as a wicked sin or crime; and its connotations are unfavourable. Shakespeare uses it in this unfavourable connotation, and we may accept here that

lust is set in opposition to *spirit*; the desires of the flesh are opposed
to the loftier possibilities of humankind, and the former can lead
to the destruction and waste of the latter. *Action*, although an
abstract word, has physical implications since action is usually
expressed through physical movement or activity. Although relatively neutral in its connotations, action can be set in opposition
to thought, for people often act before they think. Hence *action*
may suggest a degree of thoughtlessness or carelessness, and this
may be implied in this sonnet. The occurrence of *expence*, which
can imply thoughtless activity leading to wastefulness, suggests
that the *action* of line 2 is indeed one which occurs without
proper consideration. It is more likely to be importunate.

In the first two lines both *spirit* and *lust* have religious connotations, although neither is given a specifically religious denotation
here. The spirit is not said to be the human soul any more than
lust is said to be a Christian sin. In the last line of the sonnet
there are references to *heauen* and *hell*. Although both words
are of Christian and religious association, they are used here
metaphorically to suggest general happiness and well-being as
compared with misery and wretchedness. The verb *leads* has a
link with the noun *action*, because both imply activity. There is
thus a close link in the association of the words at the beginning
and end of the sonnet. Although the sonnet ostensibly describes
only human action, that action is to be judged against Christian
values though those values are implied rather than stated in the
sonnet. It is difficult to think of *lust* and *spirit* without bearing
in mind their occurrence in Christian writings, particularly the
Authorised Version of the Bible. However, there is an interesting
difference between the words in the opening lines and those in the
last line. The words at the beginning are all abstract words, though
they can have physical implications. Shakespeare suggests physical
sin without referring to any physical behaviour. But *heauen* and
hell are concrete or at least represented physical realities for most
Elizabethans, but they imply abstract qualities here.

Lines 3 and 4 contain a series of adjectives, and although the
connotations of these words are all unfavourable, for they refer
to activities which are wrong and potentially sinful, they are not
so clearly linked with religious behaviour. A participial adjective
like *periurd* has legal and possible political connotations, though
it can also be applied to humankind's obligations to God. It is,

however, a word which normally refers to human beings rather than to abstracts like *lust*, and it therefore implies that it is the human indulging in the lust who is perjured. Because it has legal associations, it further suggests that a man has a contract with God to protect his spirit, which is broken if he indulges in lust. It further suggests that the man also has a contract with the woman with whom he enjoys his lust, and that he may be deceiving her through this action. Neither contract is necessarily a written one; such contracts are understood rather than committed to writing. This in no way nullifies their force and reality. Murder is also a crime in a legal sense as well as being a sin. To murder something is to destroy it wrongfully. Thus it may be assumed that to expend spirit is the equivalent of murdering one's soul. Lust is a form of murder, for what should be guarded has been destroyed unnecessarily. Murder is also something which is linked with animate beings, for normally only something which has life may be murdered and thus lose its life. This adjective helps also to create the feeling that both spirit and lust are physical and human. Indeed, many of the adjectives in these two lines are more customarily applied to humans than to abstract entities, but it is not necessary to go through each in detail. What is important is to understand the denotative and connotative meanings of words to understand how a poet can create various levels of meaning.

It is possible to isolate the connotations of words more formally through what is known as feature analysis. This is a method of tabulating the individual features which go to make up a given word, and it helps to show in which features a word differs from others. Features are formulated as being either + or − ; that is the feature is either part of the word (+) or not (−). A *man* can be thought of as + *male*, + *human*, + *adult* and so on. As a word it shares most of these features with *woman* except that of + *male*, since *woman* can be described as − *male* or + *female*. It shares many of its features with *boy*, except that *boy* is − *adult*. It also shares many of the features with *bull*, except *bull* is − *human*. This method may be helpful in the initial stages of analysing vocabulary, for it may suggest less obvious parallelisms and contrasts.

In any literary work it is always important to bear in mind the use of proper nouns. In most forms of discourse we think of these nouns as providing the specific details required. In literature proper nouns are frequently introduced for their associative value, and some writers use them more than others. They also have a rhythm and dignity which are less felt in common nouns. A proper noun carries with it immediate echoes which may be less easy to harness with common ones. In Sonnet 129 we can assume that *spirit* and *lust* have Christian and moral associations, but that is implicit rather than explicit. Reference to a Christian event would make the frame of reference perfectly clear. Where writers wish to establish a contrast between their own times and those of some previous age it may be important for them to use proper nouns so that the contrast does not escape the reader. The use of such names provides the writers with a short, but direct, way of establishing a particular link or tone. There are none in Sonnet 129, though there are many in *Mansfield Park*. There is a subtle graduation in the names of the three sisters, from Miss Maria Ward, to Miss Ward, and finally to Miss Frances. Sir Thomas Bertram is given his full title, and his residence is stated to be *Mansfield Park, in the county of Northampton*. It acquires thereby a dignity and solidity which match the surprise that the onlookers express at the greatness of the match. His bride after all is described as no more than *Miss Maria Ward of Huntingdon*. The names highlight the difference in status. The importance of proper nouns should never be overlooked.

5 Sounds and Patterns

Syntax and lexis have been considered in the previous chapters to illustrate some of the normal principles of ordering and selection in English so that the way in which authors could adapt the norms to suit their own expressive ends was illuminated. The discussion was inevitably somewhat formal and grammatical and treated each unit within a sentence independently and without regard to other units within the same sentence. The next step is to investigate how these features are exploited as part of the wider organisation of language within literature, how the choice in one unit may influence that in another. In this chapter I shall consider how sounds and patterns are deployed within and across sentences. For example, it may be true that a particular sound is thought to evoke a given sensation or emotion: as compared with the so-called consonants like /k/ or /g/, the sound represented by the letter *s* or by *c* in the neighbourhood of front vowels is widely believed to be soft and to conjure up images of gentleness and sweetness. Hence the word *soft* itself might be selected by an author precisely because she believes its initial /s/ creates the necessary sound effect for the meaning which the word as a whole implies. But if /s/ does invoke that atmosphere associated with softness, then it is likely that an author will want to have several words in a line or sentence with the same sound or one which is close enough to it to be identified with it. So phrases like *the soft silence* or *the sweet silvery sentence* will intensify the atmosphere because of the larger number of examples of the sound. It is not necessary that the sound should come at the beginning of a word; it may make its contribution to the overall effect whatever its position in a word. Consequently there may be times when the choice of words or the organisation of the parts of a sentence is determined as much by the sound effect as by the sense. In Sonnet 129 the choice of the words in the first line may have been influenced by the wish to create a series of /s/ sounds and sounds closely related to it, including /sp/ in *expence* and *spirit*, /st/ in *waste*, /s/ in *expence*, and /sh/ in *shame*.

Sounds are divided into vowels and consonants. The vowels are made by altering the shape of the lips and the position of the tongue, but by leaving a sufficiently large gap that the air flowing out of the lungs can proceed unimpeded through the mouth. Because of this continuous stream of air which produces vowel sounds, they are often thought to be more mellifluous than consonants. Consonants are produced by blocking the airstream either entirely or so closely that the air has to be pushed out through a small aperture. The first group of consonants is called stops, because the air is stopped in its progress from the lungs out of the mouth. The second is called continuants, because the air does continue in one movement even if it has to be forced out. Consonants are felt to be harsher and more forceful than vowels because of the way in which they are made. Many English words of Anglo-Saxon origin are monosyllabic and they frequently end in a consonant, such as *good*, *bad*, *book*, *hat* and *duck*. Because words of this type have a consonant-vowel-consonant (CvC) structure, they are often considered to be less sonorous than words which end in a vowel or which have more than one syllable. If you put two such words together, then you get a clash of consonants as the final consonant of one word comes up against the initial consonant of the next. In *bad book* the /d/ of *bad* precedes the /b/ of *book*, and the phrase is difficult to pronounce without making a pause between the two words. They do not flow easily together, and that is why they are considered harsh. Furthermore, most monosyllabic words in English which are lexical words are likely to carry stress so that a phrase like *bad book* would have not only a clash of consonants, but also a juncture of two stresses which would be considered heavy. Ease of utterance usually comes with the variation of stressed and unstressed syllables. This variation occurs in polysyllabic words, and as many of the words borrowed from languages like Latin and French are polysyllabic, this variation in stress has been considered an additional advantage in introducing such words into the language.

Because so much reading today is silent, the effect of sound may seem less noticeable than it was when reading aloud was the norm. Even today some aspects of sound are immediately recognised by silent readers, the foremost of these being rhyme. There are several types of rhyme, though rhyme is usually understood to mean that basic kind in which in a stressed final syllable the root vowel (or diphthong) and the following consonant or consonants (if any) are identical in two words. Hence *boot* rhymes with *root*, because the vowel and the final consonant are identical in each word. In many forms of poetry it is the final word in a line which will rhyme, though what it rhymes with will depend upon the metre and stanza of the work in question. Except with elaborate stanzas, one line is likely to rhyme with the immediately following one or with the next but one. Rhyme patterns are represented schematically by the alphabet so that starting with *a* each line rhyming with the first line will be marked *a*, and the second rhyme and all its partners will all be marked *b*, and so on. The rhyming pattern of Sonnet 129 is therefore ababcdcdefefgg; that is, three quatrains with alternate rhyming lines and a final rhyming couplet.

Rhyme puts certain words into an emphatic position because there is a natural tendency to stress the rhyming word in a line. Rhyme also encourages the sense that each line is a complete unit of sense so that there is a pause at each line end. This tendency has been undermined in more recent poetry in which there has been a conscious attempt to downplay the feeling that each line should contain a unified syntactic unit. In Sonnet 129 it is not the case that each line represents a clause, but each line tends to have a complete sense unit within it. The first line contains the complete subject. In the second line the subject occurs at the end with the predicator on the next line. In each case this puts emphasis upon the subject. In more recent poetry the subject itself may be divided between lines in a way that would have been inconceivable in the past so that it might, for example, be possible to have *waste of* at the end of one line and *shame* on the next. In this type of poetry grammatical words can be thrust into the rhyming position; in older poetry the majority of rhyming words will be nouns or verbs. Because they are generally lexical words the rhyming words are likely to be significant in the meaning of the poem and they can provide important echoes through the poem. The occurrence of *shame* as the first rhyming word in Sonnet 129 creates the tone for the sonnet as a whole and its rhyme with *blame* merely reinforces the moral stance taken. Indeed, most of the other rhyming words in the sonnet have connotations of wickedness, misfortune and excess: *lust*, (*not to*) *trust*, *bayt*, *mad*, *extreame*, *wo* and *hell*. The others – *straight*, *had*, *so*, *dreame* and *well* – are relatively neutral. To look through those with unfavourable connotations establishes the overall meaning of the poem in a nutshell: *shame, lust, blame, bayt, mad, extreame, hell*; the stages of depravity and its results can be deduced from these words alone.

Rhyme is not the only method available for the production of sound effects in literature. Another important one is alliteration, by which the initial sound of a word (or the initial sound of its first stressed syllable) is repeated as the initial sound of other words either within the same sentence or occasionally across the sentence boundary. Since there is a tendency in English to stress the initial syllable of a word, many people feel that alliteration is more natural to the language than rhyme. Certainly alliteration was the method used in Old English, as in most other Germanic languages, as the basic principle of poetic composition. The influence of Old English techniques has surfaced from time to time in more modern poets, such as Gerard Manley Hopkins. Quite apart from this influence, alliteration has always remained a potent possibility in the language to emphasise a witticism, to join together a doublet or to make an aphorism more memorable. The proverbial utterance 'Time and tide waits for no man' exhibits the attractiveness of alliteration in the doublet '*t*ime and *t*ide', which has helped to keep *tide* alive in its old meaning. The alliteration renders the doublet tauter, and it is often used to emphasise parallelism as here, or contrast within an utterance.

In Sonnet 129 alliteration features both as a decoration and as a support for such syntactic arrangements as parallelism and contrast. In the final line the contrast between *heauen* and *hell* is accentuated by the alliteration on *h*. In lines 6–7 the parallelism in

Past reason hunted, and no sooner had
Past reason hated

is accentuated by the alliteration of /h/ in *hunted*, *had* and *hated*. This sound figures again in the tenth line, where *had*, *hauing* and *haue* are put in a sequential relationship. Other examples which bring out the parallelism include *pursut*: *possession* and *before*: *behind*, and also possibly *sooner*: *straight*, though the echo of

/s/ and /str/ is not so immediately striking. This is because when one consonantal sound is followed by another the force of the echo is only really significant when both sounds are the same. The same applies to *spirit* and *shame*, which might be thought as alliterating words because in writing both begin with *s*. But initial /sh/ is quite a different sound from that of initial /s/. Another example of alliteration which seems in this case to be more decorative than significant is *blouddy*: *blame* where the initial *bl-* is very marked. The same applies to examples of initial *pr-* which occur in *proofe*, *proud* and *proposd*. Alliteration, like rhyme, helps to bring certain words into juxtaposition by the chiming of the identical sounds and it consequently suggests that there may be links between such words which are not immediately apparent through their meaning.

Unlike rhyme, alliteration is found in prose though it may not be exploited so much there because the language of prose is not usually so ornate as that of poetry. In the opening of *Mansfield Park* there are touches of alliteration which highlight some of the implications of the story. In the first sentence, for example, there are '*r*aised to the *r*ank', '*c*omforts and *c*onsequences', and '*h*andsome *h*ouse'. Some of the features of a fortunate marriage receive special prominence by the alliteration which is used to describe them.

Rhyme and alliteration are more immediately noticeable than some other sound effects exploited by writers. Assonance and consonance, which are a kind of half-rhyme, are also frequently found in poetry, but less so in prose. Assonance is the repetition of the vowel sound without the repetition of the following consonant(s). In Sonnet 129 it could be said that *bayt* and *layd* as well as *men* and *hell* exhibit assonance. Consonance is when the consonants are identical, but not the vowel. In its full form the consonants both before and after the vowel sound are identical, but in its less striking form only the consonant(s) after the vowel sound are the same. In Sonnet 129 *hunted* and *hated* share the consonant configuration of *h – t(ed)*, but *layd* and *mad* have only the same final consonant. In the opening of the sonnet there is consonance between the /st/ of *waste* and *lust*. Finally, sound echo is achieved in ways that vary from full rhyme to the repetition of an identical or similar sound. In this instance by full rhyme I mean words rhyming together which occur in positions different from those arising in accordance with the demands of the metre or stanza organisation. At the beginning of lines 9 and 10 the words *mad* and *had* rhyme together, but the beginning of a line is not a position where rhyme is normally expected. Full rhyme may also occur at the beginning or middle or a word rather than, as usual, in its final syllable. For example, *periurd* and *murdrous* in line 3 of Sonnet 129 share the rhyme in *-urd*, though in *periurd* it occurs in the final syllable whereas in *murdrous* it occurs in the first syllable. Although a full rhyme, this example is very far from being a standard one. Line 3 of this sonnet divides into two parts, the first part being united by the rhyme on *-urd* and the second being united by the alliteration on *bl-*. Similarly in line 8 *make* and *taker* rhyme, but would not normally be regarded as a rhyming pair because *taker* rhymes on its first rather than its second syllable. In this line *make* rhymes with *taker*, but alliterates with *mad* so that there is a cross pattern of sound effects. Naturally an echo effect can also be achieved by the repetition of unstressed syllables, such as inflexional endings. In the sonnet the ending *-ed/-d* occurs throughout and accentuates some of the contrasts in it. In particular *inioyd* is paired against *dispised*, and *hunted* against *hated*; and in both cases the echo brings the contrast into greater focus because it accentuates the syntactic parallelism.

The sound effects of any piece of writing are intimately related with the stress pattern of English, which in turn underlies the metrical structure in poetry and the rhythms of prose. It is not possible to examine the bases of metre in English here. It is a convention that a line of verse can be divided into a regular number of stressed syllables and that each stressed syllable has a regular number of unstressed syllables to match it. The number of stressed syllables in a line provides the basic type of metre, so that five stressed syllables gives a pentameter line. But stress in English is not nearly so clear cut as in some other languages, and it may be difficult to determine which words are stressed in a given line of poetry. Generally lexical words carry stress, and grammatical words do not. Typically metres tend to have each stressed syllable separated by one unstressed syllable, though metres where each stressed syllable is separated by two unstressed syllable also occur. Unfortunately English does not fall easily into the pattern of x – x – because it has so many monosyllabic words, which if they are lexical will carry stress. The words in the group *high noon* would normally both be stressed, even if the first stress was less marked than the second. In the eighteenth century poets relied on bisyllabic modifiers to circumvent this difficulty and in many cases they introduced new modifiers. Hence a group like *finny tribe* produces a sequence of – x – through the use of the ending in -*y* which we regard as so characteristic of this period. The demands of the metre may influence the choice of words and the organisation of syntax.

The metre used in a poem sets up an expectation on the part of the reader or listener that the pattern will be preserved throughout the poem. It would make a poem too stereotyped if this did in fact happen and so the metrical pattern will be varied. When this happens the expectations of the reader are thwarted and the break in the pattern often throws greater emphasis on the words or group where this happens. In Sonnet 129 the basic metre is a pentameter with fived stressed syllables per line. The standard line consists of ten syllables so that there is a pattern of each stressed syllable being separated by one unstressed syllable. Line 8 exhibits this pattern:

```
x  – x   –  x –   x – x   –
```
On purpose layd to make the taker mad.

Many lines do not fall into this pattern either because they may have only four stresses, as appears to be the case in the first line where the four nouns are stressed, or because there is a junction of stressed syllables with no intervening unstressed syllable, as is the case with line 4. In that line the series of bisyllabic words turns suddenly into monosyllabic ones, though it is possible that *cruell* was understood as bisyllabic. But *extreame* has the stress on the second element, *rude* is stressed as a monosyllable, and *cruell* has a single stressed syllable (or if understood as bisyllabic would be stressed on the first element). By either interpretation it appears as though in this line three stressed syllables occur together without an intervening unstressed syllable. This has the effect of slowing down the pace of the line as well as throwing these words into emphasis, which is heightened by the assonance of *rude* and *cruell*. A similar clash of stresses is found at the beginning of line 10, where *had* and the first element of *hauing* are both stressed and thrown into prominence by the alliteration and assonance. In this line there is a sequence of three unstressed syllables -*ing, and in* – a quickening of the tempo of the line which may be intended to show the feverish nature of the quest.

In prose there is no metre, but there is rhythm. The rhythm of English has been exploited by many writers. Perhaps the most famous example is the Authorised Version of the Bible (1611), whose authors seem to have been particularly sensitive to rhythm, which is one reason why that translation has retained its appeal over so many centuries. In the Latin rhetorical tradition three standard ways of finishing a sentence were recommended in order to finish a sentence off with a rhythmical *cursus*. These three were known as *cursus planus*, *cursus tardus*, and *cursus velox* and took the following forms:

1 planus – x x (x) – x e.g. countless misfortunes; (re)markable adventure
2 tardus – x x (x) – x x e.g. vision of memory; secrets of philosophy
3 velox – x x – x – x e.g. suitable Christmas presents.

In the cursus velox the second stressed syllable may be more weakly stressed than the other two stresses. Two things are clear from the above examples. The first is that in order to achieve the necessary pattern of stressed and unstressed syllables, it is essential to use foreign loan words, usually those of Latin origin. The second follows on from that, because the words needed to form these patterns are almost always nouns of foreign origin which have to be arranged in a noun group. The result of the cursus is to throw great emphasis on the end of a sentence and hence to emphasise the end-focus within a sentence. Because of the number of monosyllabic words of Anglo-Saxon origin, this system is not very suitable for many varieties of English and tends to be found in those styles which aim for a certain heightening. Sentences with many words of Anglo-Saxon origin do not so readily end with un-stressed syllables. However, the omission of the final unstressed syllable in the planus and velox types of cursus would produce patterns more in tune with a less ornate English. Thus groups like *shimmer of light* and *depths of despair* reproduce the cursus planus without the final unstressed syllable.

Because of its reliance on a simpler style, the cursus is not very prominent in modern prose. It is found in earlier prose works, though apart from some writers in the eighteenth century its use is kept within strict limits. However, a glance at the opening paragraph of *Mansfield Park* will reveal that many of its sentences exhibit one or other of the cursus patterns. The first ends with a cursus planus: *house and large income*. The second ends with the expanded form of the cursus tardus: *equitable claim to it*. The third reverts to the cursus planus pattern: *equal advantage*; and the fourth is an example of the expanded cursus planus: *women to deserve them*. The fifth and sixth sentences break this pattern and do not exhibit any example of the cursus. But the narrative at this point departs from the even expectation of the opening to paint a rather less happy picture. It is not unreasonable that the rhythm of the language should reflect that state of affairs by being less smooth and rhythmical than that of the earlier sentences. This emphasis on the end of sentences can be taken a step further by making the patterns identical or by letting the final unstressed syllable have the same inflexional ending (*similiter cadens*) or the same sound (*similiter desinens*). For example, the two noun groups *committee of ladies* and *cremation of bodies* both end with the same ending *-ies* and this similarity can be used to point the contrast between the two groups. On the other hand, *web of corruption* and *rash of deception* both end with the same sound represented by the spelling *-tion*, and these two groups would if put in a sequence be thought to be even more closely parallel because of that link.

This similarity leads on naturally to a consideration of the construction of syntactic and other patterns in language, most of which are covered by the concept of classical rhetoric. But one pattern stands rather apart from those of rhetoric, and that is the arrangement of a number of words or groups in a sequence – a stylistic device which is commonly exploited for a variety of effects. In Sonnet 129 this can be seen most clearly in the two long complements which end the first sentence and begin the second, and it is necessary to quote lines 3–12 again:

3 Is periurd, murdrous, blouddy full of blame,
4 Sauage, extreame, rude, cruell, not to trust,
5 Inioyd no sooner but dispised straight,
6 Past reason hunted, and no sooner had

7   Past reason hated as a swollowed bayt,
8   On purpose layd to make the taker mad.
9   Mad In pursut and in possession so,
10 Had, hauing and in quest to haue extreame,
11 A blisse in proofe and proud and very wo,
12 Before a ioy proposd behind a dreame.

The first complement (lines 3–8) consists of four parts which each have their organisational pattern: a list of modifiers (3–4), two participial phrases set in contrast (5), two participial phrases which are parallel (6–7), and an image (7–8) which may refer just to the previous parallelism, but which could refer both to that and to the preceding contrast. It is more satisfactory to think of lines 5–8 being made up of three items, the first two of which are parallel with each other and the third expands on both items at the beginning. These lines together then form a unit which is set against the unit consisting of the series of modifiers in lines 3–4. Although the list of modifiers is somewhat heavy, it is not as heavy as the series of interlocking contrasts and parallelisms which make up lines 5–8. The list of modifiers naturally consists of a series in itself, which contains a succession of linking devices. The first two are linked by the echo of -urd, the second two by the alliteration on bl-, the third two are both bisyllabic, the fourth two are linked by assonance, and the final modifier echoes the syntactic organisation of the modifier at the end of the previous line. Semantically there is not much evidence of a progression in meaning among these modifiers, which are held together more by sound and rhythm than by meaning. In all parts of the overall series it is in general balance which is important rather than progression, even though often in a series there is a natural tendency to go from lighter to heavier weight to prevent any sense of bathos or anti-climax.

The second complement has much the same structure in that it relies more on balance than progression. It too consists of four parts: in this case each occupies a single line. Line 9 has two items parallel to each other linked by alliteration; line 10 has three items in a series also linked by alliteration and assonance; line 11 has a series of three items, two of which share alliteration on pr-; and line 12 contains two items set in a contrastive relationship and linked by the alliterative echo on be-. These four parts of the series fall into a pattern themselves, since the first and the last consist of two items each, whereas the second and the third consist of three items each.

In classical times rhetoric was a means whereby what one had to say, particularly in forensic oratory, was organised in the most telling manner. It dealt with all aspects of organisation and presentation of spoken or written language. Over the years, however, rhetoric came increasingly to be associated with figures of speech and hence to be criticised as a way of decorating language in an unnecessary and artificial way. Even so books promoting rhetorical techniques have been published in all centuries and many writers reveal in their work the attractions of the figures. This is hardly surprising since the precepts embody ways in which language can be made more persuasive and powerful. As a first step it may be helpful to give a list of some of the more commonly found figures. The names they are known by vary from one writer to the next, and I have used those which occur most regularly.

Anadiplosis	The final word or words of a clause or sentence repeated as the first word or words of the next clause or sentence.
Anaphora	A series of clauses, sentences or lines of a poem each commencing with the same word.
Antanaclasis	The repetition of a word in a different sense from that in which it was first used.
Antimetabole	The repetition of two or more words in inverse order from that in which they first occurred.
Asyndeton	A series of words or phrases joined together with no linking conjunctions.
Epanalepsis	The repetition of the same word or words at the beginning and end of a sentence or clause.
Epistrophe	The repetition of the same word at the end of a series of clauses or sentences.
Epizeuxis	The same word or phrase repeated immediately.
Isocolon	The balance of clauses or sentences of equal length.
Parison	The use of identical structure in a series of groups or clauses so that there is an echo in each group or clause of adjective to adjective, noun to noun, etc.
Paronomasia	The repetition of words with a similar sound but a different sense.

Ploce	The repetition of the same word within a line of poetry or within a series of clauses.
Polyptoton	The repetition of a word with a change in its inflexional ending, such as *walks: walking*.
Syllepsis	The use of a word in one sense but suggesting that another sense of that word is also relevant in the context.
Zeugma	The use of a single verb with two or more complements, particularly where that verb may suggest a different meaning is foremost with each complement.

We can now see how some of these figures are exploited in Sonnet 129. First we can isolate the different figures and then evaluate how they contribute to the overall effect of the sonnet. The first line contains several examples of syllepsis. In particular *waste* in the sense of barren desert also conjures up *waist* as an object of sexual desire in its physical human sense. The link between sexual experience and sterility is made at the beginning of the sonnet. But *expence* also has a dual sense, the first being the expenditure of effort and the second the cost in financial and other terms. Even *spirit* suggests both physical effort and the soul. The first line also contains an example of parison since the two groups have an identical structure of article, noun, *of* and noun. This parison supplements the syllepsis in confirming that there is an immediate relationship between sexual lust and barrenness of the soul.

The second line contains an example of antimetabole, for the two words *lust* and *action* are repeated in a reverse order. This enables *lust* to come almost at the beginning of the line and at its end so that it becomes an example of epanalepsis. Lines 2 and 3 both begin with the same word *is* and so constitute an example of anaphora; another example is the repetition of *past* at the beginning of lines 6 and 7. Lines 3 and 4 illustrate asyndeton or the heaping up of a series of words or groups without any linking conjunction. Both lines end with a similar structure different from the rest of each line and they form another example of parison. The phrases *past reason hunted* and *past reason hated* are examples of anaphora, parison and isocolon as well as illustrating paronomasia through the echo *hunted/hated*. The coming together of so many rhetorical figures in these lines highlights the speed with which lust turns into loathing. The second and third quatrains are linked by an example of anadiplosis, for *mad* ends line 8 and begins line 9. This word also exemplifies syllepsis, for it means both 'driven to excess' and 'foolish, out of one's mind'. In line 9 *in pursuit* and *in possession* exemplify parison, and the following line contains an example of polyptoton in that it exhibits three forms of the verb 'to have': the infinitive *haue*, the present participle *hauing*, and the past participle *had*. This past participle form *had* is found in line 6 and is repeated here as an example of ploce, as is true of *extreame* found in this line and line 4. Line 11 introduces a series of contrasts which are not examples of rhetorical figures as such, but which carry on the taut structure of the sonnet: *blisse:wo*; *before: behind*; *heauen: hell*. In line 12 *before a ioy* and *behind a dreame* constitute an example of parison, and *before* and *behind* may well be examples of syllepsis since they imply both time and place. In line 13 there is an example of antimetabole since *well knowes* is repeated in inverse order as *knowes well*.

The rhetorical figures combine with the metrical, rhythmical and sound patterns to produce a taut, interlaced verbal organisation which is strikingly effective and memorable. The figures concentrate the mind on certain words and concepts to drive home the message of the sonnet as a whole. In no sense can they be considered to be purely decorative; they are part of the message. Inevitably, the figures of rhetoric are more likely to be found in poetry than in prose, particularly in shorter poems in which a concentration of the vocabulary through various patternings is aimed at. Prose is more expansive and so does not need the intense organisation of language which rhetoric encourages. Some figures do occur in many prose styles. In *Mansfield Park* the emphasis on money is indicated through the ploce on *thousand*. The rhythm of the prose may be accentuated by parison as happens with the identical adjective-noun structure of 'handsome house and large income'. Anaphora may also occur, as in the use of *Miss Ward* to commence sentences 5 and 6. Syllepsis is found in those authors like Jane Austen who exploit its possibilities for irony. In the opening sentence the use of *captivate* has not only the sense of 'enthrall through her charms and beauty', but also the less agreeable sense of 'capture'. The word *attached* can also be understood in two ways: its apparent meaning is little more than 'married', but it also implies 'joined (in a somewhat unsatisfactory manner)' for *attached* seems to contradict the *equal* of 'equal advantage' which is introduced a couple of sentences earlier. A form of asyndeton occurs in 'her uncle, the lawyer, himself', for the latter two elements in the series are unnecessary as far as the reader's understanding of what is going on is concerned. Ploce is also found with the adjectives in 'handsome house and large income' repeated in 'quite as handsome as Miss Maria' and 'men of large fortune'. The word 'fortune' is itself repeated elsewhere in the passage. All of these examples help to create the tone of the passage which is so important for our understanding and enjoyment of the novel.

6 Pragmatics and Literary Texts

In this book so far I have been dealing with aspects of language within a sentence, though it was noted in the previous chapter that sound and metre could, and often do, operate beyond the confines of a single sentence. In this and the following chapter I wish to consider those elements of a text which go beyond the sentence and provide the cement which unites individual utterances into a single text. A sentence may be grammatically correct in so far as it observes the syntactic and lexical rules of English, but it may be unintelligible because the grammatical elements do not combine to produce a meaningful statement in the English language. The sentence proposed by Noam Chomsky to illustrate this concept was 'Colourless green ideas sleep furiously'. This utterance contains the clause elements (SPA) in a pattern which is syntactically quite acceptable in English, but the lexical elements do not combine together to produce a statement which makes any sense to most English people. Equally it is possible to have two sentences which are juxtaposed which individually may be meaningful, but which together appear not to be. For example, the two sentences 'He went shopping in Sainsbury's every Monday for his wife. The government in Afghanistan has collapsed in the face of continued rebel attacks.' appear to be quite unrelated and so they would not normally constitute a coherent text. It may be possible to invent a situation in which these two sentences could be thought to form a coherent sequence, such as possibly the headline in a local radio station's news broadcast though even that seems a little dubious. In this chapter I shall deal with some of the presuppositions which lie behind many utterances and so provide an almost hidden means of linking them into a meaningful sequence. In the next chapter I shall deal with some of the more apparent devices which help to unite utterances into a coherent text.

The general aim of pragmatics can be said to be the study of meaning in language which arises from its contextual situation as distinct from its grammatical organisation, though a watertight definition of pragmatics is extremely difficult to provide. To some extent the domain of pragmatics is determined by how one approaches meaning and semantics, but this is a problem which cannot be tackled here. It will be sufficient for our purposes to focus on the meaning which is inherent in the contextual situation, which can vary very widely. For example, an utterance can change from being a question to a threat if the context warrants that interpretation. A question such as 'Are you going to give me the money?' could easily be understood as a threat in certain contexts. It is important to realise that it is the context which determines the most acceptable meaning of the utterance. Several factors are important in determining how the context influences the meaning of a given utterance, and these will be considered in turn.

The first factor is presupposition, for every utterance we make presupposes cultural and other knowledge to enable us to understand what is said properly and fully. Presupposition can vary from the factual to the intangible. Consider, for example, a short dialogue as follows:

A: I have a headache.
B: There is some paracetamol upstairs.

A purely concrete presuppostion behind B's statement is that paracetamol is a medicine which is frequently taken to cure headaches. Clearly someone who was unaware of this would make little sense of the response. But this presupposition is little more than an understanding of the vocabulary, including the technical vocabulary, of a language. A second presupposition which is also mainly concrete, though it has cultural elements in it as well, concerns the concept 'upstairs'. B's response makes sense only in those countries where the normal residence consists of an upstairs as well as a downstairs. In those countries where the normal residence was either a bungalow or a flat a reader or listener might have trouble making sense of the concept 'upstairs'. Indeed, the presupposition goes further. In Britain it is normal to have an upstairs and a downstairs, and so there is little or no implication of status involved in having an upstairs. But in some countries it could well be that whereas most people lived on one floor only, the very rich or powerful had two or more floors in their homes. If this were so, then there could be a presupposition in this statement as to the status of the speakers. For most people the upstairs of B's statement is almost certain to be interpreted as meaning the bathroom since the most usual place to keep medicines is in the bathroom cupboard. That presupposes that the bathroom is itself upstairs.

A less tangible presupposition concerns the relationship of the two speakers. One could expand B's statement along the following lines to make the presuppositions in it more explicit. 'If you have a headache, then you could take a paracetamol tablet. We have some tablets upstairs in the bathroom. I therefore suggest that you go upstairs to the bathroom to get one or two of the tablets. You could then take it (or them) with a glass of water, and if you do that you should feel better shortly.' In other words various actions are presupposed in B's statement, and these actions presuppose a relationship between the two speakers. In general one would assume that they were both of roughly equal status. One would not expect one to be a parent and the other a child, if only because most parents spend a lot of their time and energy keeping medicines out of the reach of children. To encourage children to take medicines for themselves even for such a trivial thing as a headache is not likely for most parents. Equally it is not likely that A is an aged parent and B an adult son or daughter, since one would normally not wish to impose a journey upstairs on someone for whom such a trip could be tiring or even painful. Similarly it is unlikely that A is the mistress of a household and B a servant within it, for one would not expect a servant to advise the mistress to do something herself if the servant could reasonably and easily do it for her. However, in this case it would be possible for A to be the servant and B the mistress of the house.

Presupposition may also be helpful in indicating genre and this applies particularly to various types of literary genre. Imagine a different dialogue along these lines:

A: Did you sleep well?
B: No. There was an elephant in my bed.

For most people this conversation would be impossible since in no human culture known to me does an elephant sleep in a bed. A dialogue of this sort is possible only where there is a suspension of the normal conditions of human and animal life, as is characteristic of certain genres. Hence if the dialogue is to be understood as meaningful it must belong to such a genre. The most likely is that of children's literature, which makes use of fantasy and breaks the expectations of everyday life. Fairy tales are now virtually a part of children's literature. Some other types of fantasy literature, not excluding science fiction, could also contain a dialogue of this sort readily enough.

We have seen already that dialogue may presuppose the status or relationship of the speakers involved, and this is a point that merits a little further discussion since it will lead on to the second factor in the contextual situation. Certain utterances are unlikely to be used by people of differing status or, if they do occur, will be found only within a dialogue rather than at its inception. For example, if I see my postman from time to time and notice one day that he has shaved off his beard I am unlikely to open my conversation when I meet him that day with 'I see you have shaved off your beard'. To make this statement implies a degree of familiarity between the two participants of the dialogue, and that degree is not one which I have with my postman. Although one might talk to the postman about the weather, which is a daily phenomenon, one is less likely to talk about something more personal such as shaving off a beard. The reason for this is that a beard cannot be shaved off everyday and so a statement such as 'I see you have shaved off your beard' may well be understood as a question 'Why have you shaved off your beard?' At least the statement would usually be answered by an explanation as to why the beard was missing and this shows that the person addressed would understand the statement to call for some explanatory response. It is because an explanation is implicitly demanded that speakers who are not too familiar with each other would hesitate before making a statement of this sort. Or at least they would not introduce their dialogue in this way, though if the dialogue extended beyond the pleasantries of the day they might feel sufficiently confident to introduce it at some later stage in the exchange.

This example introduces the second factor in the contextual situation which may be broadly categorised under the heading speech act. A speech act can be understood as an act performed by the speaker towards the person addressed and there are various kinds of acts into which utterances fit. This formal aspect of speech act theory is less important for stylistics than some of the other features of speech performance. For instance, there is a relation between what is said and the syntactic means used to express it. There are three major forms of sentence structure in English: declarative (or statement), interrogative (or question), and imperative (or command). It is possible to express most acts in all of these three ways, though the implication socially and linguistically may well be different in each case. Thus if you want the person you are with to leave you, it is possible to say

1 Go away. (imperative)
2 Isn't it time for you to leave? (interrogative)
3 It is time for you to leave. (declarative)

As a general rule each syntactic structure carries with it a certain force, and it is that force which is often significant within stylistics. Imperatives usually have more force than interrogatives, and interrogatives more than declaratives. The force of any syntactic structure can be modified in many ways. The addition of a form of address, such as a name or title, or of a politeness formula, such as *please*, will normally reduce the force of an utterance. 'Please go away' has less force than 'Go away'. The addition or omission of a negative may also vary the force of an utterance. There is a difference in the force of these two statements

2a Isn't it time for you to leave?
2b Is it time for you to leave?

The second would seem to most English speakers to be nearer to a genuine enquiry than the first, which approximates more to a command than a question. In analysing texts, particularly literary texts, the force of an utterance is often more revealing than its precise speech act form.

Within speech act theory and more generally in pragmatics it has been widely accepted that conversation is based on the co-operative principle. This means that the participants in a conversation co-operate to produce a meaningful series of exchanges.

It is only on the basis of this assumption that one can understand the short dialogue given earlier in the chapter

    A: I have a headache.
    B: There is some paracetamol upstairs.

It is because we assume that B is co-operating with A in the conversation that we can interpret B's statement as being meaningful within the context. If this were not so, we would assume that the two statements were entirely unrelated to each other, because there is at first sight very little connection between them. This concept of their co-operative principle was first put forward by H. P. Grice, an American philosopher, as part of the set of general assumptions which guide our conversational strategies. The other assumptions were encapsulated as certain maxims which we observe as we talk. These are the maxims of quality, quantity, relevance and manner.

The maxim of quality is that speakers should say only what they know or believe to be true, or rather that they should not say anything for which they have no adequate evidence as to its truthfulness. The maxim of quantity states that speakers should say only as much as is needed to make their contributions to the conversation as informative as is required. They should not say more or less than is required. The maxim of relevance is that any contribution to a conversation should be relevant, i.e. that it should develop, or respond to, the contributions which had already been made. Finally the maxim of manner indicates that any contribution should be clear, unambiguous, brief and well-ordered. These four maxims can be said to represent the ideal of conversation, though most readers will realise that in many conversations some or all of the maxims are broken. And the same applies to literature. The important point to recognise is that these maxims do provide the assumptions behind any discourse. If they are broken it is important to find out the reasons. Even when a maxim is flouted, the assumption of co-operation is such that it will be accepted that the flouting is deliberate and that the contribution is meant to be co-operative. One will go out of one's way to find meaning in what seems at first sight to be a series of totally unrelated utterances. Many of the traditional figures of speech could be said to flout these maxims, and irony may also be indicated through their flouting. For example, in a conversation like

A: John's going out with Sue.
B: He's a lemon.

one would have to assume that for speaker B for a young man to go out with Sue represented 'lemon-like' behaviour. Precisely what a lemon is in this context may vary for different speakers, but then that is true for much figurative language. But B's statement breaks the maxim of relevance, because a lemon appears to bear no relation to taking Sue out.

The third factor which is relevant to the contextual situation is deixis, that is the location of an utterance to speaker, space and time. Words like *I*, *you*, *here*, *there*, *now* and *tomorrow* are all contextually significant and vary according to each speaker. In many conversations the context is implied from what is said rather than made explicit; in many poems the poet may refer to a background but the reader may not know precisely what the background is. The *I* of a poem may be the poet or it may be a fictitious entity created for the poem.

It is time now to test some of these principles against a piece of literature. In this chapter I will abandon the texts that have been used hitherto in this book, because some of the principles are better illustrated through drama, which is made up of conversation. It should not be thought that drama is the only type of literature in which pragmatic factors are important; it is merely that type in which the principles can be most readily explained. An illustration of how the principles of pragmatics can be exploited in a poem will be found in the final chapter. The text I have chosen is the opening of *Hamlet*. It is a play which is well known to most people and it is also considered 'normal' in its use of language. By that I mean that it is not usually thought to exhibit those deviations from ordinary English which are so characteristic of some modern plays, such as *Waiting for Godot* or *The Caretaker*. Furthermore, the text of *Hamlet* is available both in the First Folio of 1623 and in various quartos, including the 1603 quarto. This used to be referred to as a 'bad' quarto because it was thought to have a text based on memorial reconstruction of one or two actors. Its text is certainly quite different in important respects from that of the First Folio. To start with I reproduce the text as found in the First Folio.

Enter Barnardo and Francisco two Centinels

BARNARDO:	Who's there?
FRANCISCO:	Nay answer me: Stand & vnfold your selfe.
BAR:	Long liue the King.
FRAN:	*Barnardo*?
BAR:	He.
FRAN:	You come most carefully vpon your houre.
BAR:	'Tis now strook twelue, get thee to bed *Francisco*.
FRAN:	For this releefe much thankes: 'Tis bitter cold, And I am sicke at heart.
BARN:	Haue you had quiet Guard?
FRAN:	Not a Mouse stirring.
BARN:	Well, goodnight. If you do meet *Horatio* and *Marcellus*, The Riuals of my Watch, bid them make hast.

Enter Horatio and Marcellus

FRAN:	I thinke I heare them. Stand: who's there?	
HORATIO:	Friends to this ground.	15
MARCELLUS:	And Leige-men to the Dane.	
FRAN:	Giue you good night.	
MAR:	O farwel honest Soldier, who hath relieu'd you?	
FRA:	Barnardo ha's my place: giue you goodnight.	
	Exit Fran.	
MAR:	Holla *Barnardo*.	20
BAR:	Say, what is *Horatio* there?	
HOR:	A peece of him.	
BAR:	Welcome *Horatio*, welcome good *Marcellus*.	
MAR:	What ha's this thing appear'd againe to night.	
BAR:	I haue seene nothing.	25

The opening question by Barnardo is one which has genre restrictions on it. It tends to be used in situations where the speaker thinks there is someone present, but does not know who that person is or whether he is friendly. Consequently it has overtones of anxiety, because it is used in situations which could turn hostile, if it should turn out that the 'stranger(s)' are not friendly. Hence if I were sitting by myself in my lounge in the evening and I expected my wife back at any moment, a noise at the front door would signal to me my wife's return. I would not shout out 'Who's there?' in such a situation; I would probably say something like 'Is that you, dear?' If, on the other hand, my wife had gone away for the weekend and I was in the lounge by myself and there was a noise at the front door, I might well shout 'Who's there?' because I would expect it to be a stranger – even perhaps a burglar. If the latter was the case, then the situation could well turn nasty and violent. In other words the question 'Who's there?' has a certain hostile and apprehensive note, because the speaker is announcing that he does not know who the other person is and is probably not expecting anyone to be there in the first place. It is not a question which one might expect a relief sentry to ask the sentry on duty, because it might be assumed that sentries knew each other and were on sufficiently familiar terms to make this question unlikely. But we as audience do not yet know what is happening on the stage – if we can assume, that is, that we were seeing the play for the first time and without having read it beforehand, as would be true of the original audiences. It is clear that the author wishes to inject a note of apprehension and urgency into the scene from its beginning.

The reply is unexpected because it immediately flouts the co-operative principle. When someone is asked a direct question, then it is reasonable to expect a reply to that question. The respondent refuses to answer the question and makes a counter request for information about the original speaker. This answer is very forceful: it is introduced by *Nay* and it contains three impera-tives *answer*, *stand* and *vnfold*. There is no question of the force of these imperatives being softened by the use of a politeness formula or by any form of address. It is clear that the second speaker feels that he has a greater right to know who the original speaker is than he has an obligation to answer that speaker's question. His answer is in effect saying 'No, I will not answer you, for you must answer me. Stay where you are and reveal your identity'. Within the context of an exchange of sentries, the presupposition must be that the second speaker, Francisco, has this right because he is the sentry on duty. It is his obligation to question people who approach him and not the other way round. It is, of course, also customary for a sentry to see someone else coming before he is himself challenged, and the exchange here is unusual in that respect. It suggests that Barnardo is more alert than Francisco, and perhaps more anxious. It may be that from the dramatist's point of view he wants a more important character to speak first. This underlines a problem for drama which is not found in ordinary dialogue. Dramatists can speak to the audience only through the speech of their characters, and so may on occasion get them to say things which we as audience need to know rather than what they as characters need to say.

The opening of the play has created a sense of aggression and anxiety through the exchanges which take place. We need to remember that this is not how the exchange need have developed. A more neutral dialogue could have been along the lines:

BARNARDO: Is that you Francisco?
FRANCISCO: Yes. I'm over here.

It is when we see what a neutral exchange would look like that we realise how much tension is built into the one which Shakespeare created. The opening of the play is preparing for the frightening events which are to come. Barnardo does not reply directly to Francisco's challenge in so far as he does not reveal his name, but he says simply 'Long liue the King'. It is often thought by commentators that this is the password for the evening, but that seems unlikely because it is not used by Marcellus and Horatio when they are challenged a few minutes later. There may be some dramatic irony in Barnardo's response in so far as the king does not live long, but that is not the primary pragmatic reason for the response. The response probably has to be interpreted not as a password, but as a general reply meaning 'My business is friendly'. This in turn has an implication for the meaning of Francisco's *vnfold your selfe*. This is often taken to mean 'What is your name?', but it probably means something like 'What is your business; are you friend or foe?'; Barnardo's response is perfectly understandable if what Francisco is saying is understood properly. Pragmatics can often help interpretation at the semantic level. 'Long liue the King' is a formula which the audience accept as such, for they do not know who the king is; but the two participants in the dialogue clearly do.

To this reply Francisco says simply *Barnardo*? This reply has one difficulty in that in Elizabethan times a question mark did service to indicate not only a question, but also an exclamation. Francisco's utterance could be understood either as 'Is that Barnardo?' or as 'Then it must be Barnardo!' In view of the tone of anxiety of what precedes, the former is the more likely interpretation, for it continues the state of uncertainty a little further. Barnardo's reply to the question is *He*. This means no more than 'That's correct, I am Barnardo', but its form is unusual. There seems no reason for Barnardo to refer to himself in the third person as though he were talking about someone other than himself. It maintains a level of formality, which has been evident in the exchange so far. Neither speaker has evinced any great familiarity with the other, and their precise relationship is uncertain. Do they know each other simply as sentries, or are they more friendly? The former is the more likely interpretation on the evidence available.

Francisco now says to him 'You come most carefully vpon your houre' – a statement which has some puzzling features in it. How does Francisco know precisely what the time is? He is a soldier on the battlements of a castle in the middle of the night, as we discover later. In the early seventeenth century it would have been difficult for such people to know the precise time. If he did know the time and was expecting to be relieved at that time, it is strange that he should have been surprised by Barnardo who speaks first in the dialogue. If he was expecting Barnardo, why did he have to go through the rigmarole of the challenges to confirm that it was him? His use of the adjunct *most carefully* suggests that Barnardo is unusually precise in his arrival on that occasion, for we would never emphasise punctuality to someone who was always punctual. There is a suggestion here that Barnardo has some reason to be so punctual on that evening. The expression *vpon your houre* presupposes that Francisco was expecting someone then, because *houre* indicates some kind of appointment which has a fixed time attached to it.

Barnardo's response to this statement is difficult to interpret partly because of the punctuation in the Folio. With only a comma in the middle of *'Tis now strook twelue, get thee to bed Francisco*, one might assume that the two clauses were related with the meaning 'Because it has struck twelve, it's time for you to go to bed'. Most modern editors put a full-stop after *twelue* to make the utterance into two separate and presumably unrelated sentences. In that case Barnardo's statement *'Tis now strook twelue* has to be understood as a comment on his punctuality as remarked upon by Francisco. It would be as much as to say 'Yes I am on time because it has just struck twelve'. Normally one might expect Francisco's statement with its *most carefully* to be understood as a question asking why Barnardo had arrived so punctually that night. If that is so, then Barnardo does not pick up the lead offered by Francisco, and it could be said that he fails to co-operate with him in this stretch of dialogue. Instead of saying why he is punctual, he merely confirms that he is on time because he notes the hour. The information he provides in this way breaks the maxim of quantity because the information about the time is already presupposed in what Francisco said. The information may be of interest to the audience, since this is the first indication they have of the time of the action, but it does not tell Francisco anything new and consequently can be regarded as concealing information. Barnardo does not apparently want to inform Francisco of why he is on time that night. This flouting of the co-operative principle increases the sense of expectancy and anxiety already generated in the scene.

Barnardo then goes on to say *get thee to bed Francisco*. This statement can be said to follow on naturally from the time which has just been indicated, but I think we have to note its force. The recommendation is put in the imperative and as such has very strong force. It could have been expressed less forcefully through an interrogative such as 'Why don't you go to bed now?' The force of the imperative is designed to underline the urgency which Barnardo feels about getting Francisco out of the way. However, Barnardo tries to mitigate the force of this command in two ways: he uses *thee* and he uses the form of address *Francisco*. In order to understand the importance of *thee* it is necessary to explain briefly the difference between *thee* and *you* in Elizabethan English. Originally in English there existed a singular (*thou, thee, thine*) and a plural (*ye, you, your*) form of the second person personal pronoun. The distinction between the forms was one of number: the singular referred to only one person and the plural referred to more than one person. Gradually the plural form was extended to singular use as well so that both forms could be used in the singular. In the singular they were differentiated as to use, for the *you* forms were unmarked and neutral whereas the *thou* forms were marked and restricted in use. This distinction corresponds to that found between *tu* and *vous* in French and between *du* and *Sie* in German. *Thou* was used to express intimacy or it was addressed to an inferior; it could also be used to indicate anger or even awe, as when addressing the supernatural. Various studies have been made into Shakespeare's usage to show how he uses *thou* in marked situation. However, these studies have failed to take pragmatic force into account. It is clear that Barnardo does not use *thou* here as a general term of intimacy, for he does not use *thou* in his other speeches to Francisco. In his next two utterances to Francisco he uses only *you*, e.g. *Haue you had quiet Guard*? Equally Francisco uses only *you* to Barnardo. The apparent level of familiarity between these two characters is not such as to support the use of *thou* between them. Clearly Barnardo uses *thou* on this single occasion only to mitigate the force of his command. In other words he expresses his anxiety to get Francisco out of the way as quickly as possible by using an imperative, but he wishes to show that it is not rudeness which prompts this imperative by using the *thou* form. He supports this *thou* form by addressing Francisco by his name. This is not to inform the audience of his name, because his name is not relevant to the development of the plot or the audience's understanding of it.

Francisco does not respond to this imperative by leaving; he continues the conversation. First he thanks Barnardo for the relief he brings to his turn of duty. Since Barnardo has come at his appropriate time, this is not exceptional relief and so hardly needs particular thanks. But the thanks in this case are offered because of the nature of the night and the condition of Francisco: *'Tis bitter cold, And I am sicke at heart*. Both reasons are offered without further elaboration. To be sick at heart is not to be physically ill, but to be depressed or generally upset. Clearly within the wider framework of the play it introduces the note of sickness which figures prominently in it. Here it suggests no more than a sentry who is frozen and fed up, though it may imply more than that. Barnardo does not appear to respond directly to what Francisco has said. He does not say 'Why are you sick at heart?' But his answer can be understood to imply that because of the co-operative principle. He says *Haue you had quiet Guard?* The co-operative principle would lead us to presuppose that this question is related to the previous comment, as though Barnardo supposed that something had happened during Francisco's guard duty to make him sick at heart. In fact it turns out that Barnardo has ulterior motives for asking this question because he has arranged with others to see whether the ghost comes again, though that is not something we the audience know as yet. The statement by Francisco about his state of mind and Barnardo's response can only increase the sense that something unusual is taking place. In fact Francisco answers Barnardo's question with *Not a Mouse stirring*. This reply breaks the maxim of quantity. Francisco means simply 'Yes', but his reply is expressed as a negative and a very strong one at that. There is more information provided than is required. The suggestion is that the guard has been almost preternaturally quiet and that can only increase the sense of apprehension yet further. Equally it does not provide any information about why Francisco is sick at heart, for we can hardly assume that this quietness is the cause of his condition. Barnardo does not follow up why Francisco has this condition and so reveals that his question about the guard was not motivated primarily by his anxiety for Francisco. He is following his own line of thought.

It is because he is following his own line of thought to acquire the information he needs that he can now dismiss Francisco. Instead of enquiring further about Francisco's state of mind, he says *Well, goodnight. Good night* is always used as a sign of concluding a conversation or at parting. It is not used to introduce a conversation or in its middle. It differs in that respect from *Good morning* or *Good evening*, both of which could be used as initiating points in a dialogue. Hence Barnardo's remark can be seen only as a way of getting rid of Francisco and reinforces his earlier *get thee to bed Francisco*. This time the brusqueness of the remark is not softened by any form of address or courtesy formula. But he then adds as an afterthought the plea that if Francisco should meet Horatio and Marcellus who are to share his watch he should ask them to hurry up. Although an afterthought this request does presuppose that Francisco knows who these two people are and also suggests that he finds it acceptable that two people should share the watch with Barnardo. Both of these presuppositions are actually somewhat improbable. As we find out later Horatio has only just arrived in Denmark and as Francisco has been on watch by himself, he might reasonably think that there should be only a single sentry on duty at any time. Francisco does not question Barnardo's request. In making the request Barnardo is revealing his concern that the other two should be there as soon as possible. Since there is no apparent reason why they should be there, this concern again raises the sense of expectancy.

This comment terminates the first part of this scene. Naturally little information about the contextual situation has been provided. There is no reason why the two characters should refer to time and place since both are clear to the speakers. The place could also be clear to the audience and possibly the approximate time if the stage was in darkness, though that could not have been true on the Elizabethan stage. The only indication of time we get is that the clock has struck twelve. The characters address each other relatively formally through the use of *you*, and their precise relationship is not easy to disentangle. Generally the exchange brings out the anxiety and apprehension of the occasion, though no information is given as to that anxiety. One character is more anxious than the other and is trying to get him to leave quickly; he is also anxious that his colleagues who are named should join him as soon as possible. Much of this is presupposed rather than stated directly.

Francisco responds to this last remark of Barnardo's, saying he thinks he can hear them approaching and he then goes on to challenge them. He has evidently moved away from Barnardo before he does so, because the exchange which takes place is clearly outside his hearing. Francisco utters a simple challenge *Stand: who's there?* Although he knows who might be coming, because he has just referred to *them*, i.e. Horatio and Marcellus, he is too good a soldier to assume that it must be them. He goes through the motions of a formal challenge by asking them to halt and to disclose who they are. They respond in a way similar to that used by Barnardo earlier in the scene. Both of them speak and the second joins his remark on to that of the first. Neither discloses his name, for both use a formula-type expression to declare that their purpose is friendly. Horatio speaks first, although it turns out he is a stranger, presumably on the grounds that he is more important than Marcellus. The precise referent of *this ground* is not clear, but we assume it means the country in which they are then located. Marcellus's addition makes it clear that it is Denmark since he claims both are vassals of the King of Denmark. In this way they both establish that they are on friendly business and have a right to be there. This right is not challenged by Francisco, who accepts their claim. He does not seek to identify them further, and we presuppose that he identifies them as Horatio and Marcellus. He does not do what he was asked to do, namely to urge them to go on to Barnardo as soon as possible – an omission which may be accounted for by the fact that they are almost there anyway. What he does do is to wish them good night, which can be interpreted as a way of not delaying their arrival at the proper place. His *Giue you good night* is formal and neutral; it betrays no familiarity.

Marcellus then speaks *O farwel honest Soldier, who hath relieu'd you*? From this we understand that Marcellus does not know who the other speaker is and does not wish to establish his identity. He does, however, assume that he is a soldier and that he has just finished his turn at sentry duty. Why he makes this presupposition is not clear. If the night is dark, he would not have seen him clearly. How would he know that he had finished sentry duty? Naturally if he was a soldier rather than an officer, the completion of sentry duty is the most likely reason for him to be there, if one assumes that everyone recognised that the place at which this dialogue was taking place was not the place at which sentries should be on duty. Consequently the soldier could be there only if he was finishing his duty if he was the *honest Soldier* that Marcellus describes him as. In other words to be honest, to be an ordinary soldier, and to be finishing the sentry duty all seem to be interrelated in this statement. It is not likely that the sentry could be going to his sentry duty, because Marcellus and Horatio have come to meet Barnardo, who is starting his duty then, and because Francisco is presumably going in the opposite direction to Marcellus and Horatio, who are on the way to the sentry position. Once again the pragmatics may help us to understand the semantics, for *honest* here would best be understood from the contextual situation to mean something like 'reliable, someone who performs his duty punctiliously'. It follows also that it is because he is reliable that he would not leave his post until he had been relieved, that he would not simply vacate his post when it was time but would wait for his relief however

late he might be. The *farwel* also presupposes that because of
the direction the soldier is going in he is leaving, even though
Marcellus and Horatio have just been challenged by him. Hence
when the soldier bids them good night, it is because he is leaving
and not because Horatio and Marcellus are. The question put by
Marcellus is answered simply and straightforwardly by Francisco,
who provides the information requested. He then repeats his good
night formula and leaves without waiting for any further response.
The formula which Francisco uses twice *Giue you good night* is not
common in Shakespeare, for the *giue you* is not usually linked with
good night. Whether this means it was slightly more formal is not
clear, though that could well be so.

When Francisco leaves, Marcellus shouts out *Holla Barnardo*.
We can say he shouts out, because *Holla* is usually used to attract
attention, often over a distance. This is a friendly greeting as
compared with *Who's there?* The speaker assumes that the person
addressed is present and he merely tries to attract his attention. It
is usual in such circumstances to assume that the two speakers are
some distance apart or at least that they cannot see each other,
which in this instance could be caused by the darkness of the night.
Whether it is dark or not has not been stated by any speaker so far
though there is much in the language which presupposes that it is,
though later in this scene we learn that the stars are out. Barnardo
must recognise Marcellus's voice because he addresses the speaker
and says *Say, what is Horatio there?* He recognises the voice, but
cannot see whether there are two people there or not. He knows
that the voice was that of Marcellus and was expecting two people
to come and so he enquired whether the second person, Horatio,
has come with him. We must presuppose that the speakers are still
some way apart.

Horatio replies to Barnardo's question. He does not say something like 'Yes' or 'I'm here'. Instead he refers to himself in the
third person by saying *A peece of him*. This could have been said
by Marcellus in the third person of his companion, but we have
to assume that Barnardo recognises a different voice and deduces
that it is Horatio himself who is speaking in that way. Why does
Horatio speak of himself in the third person? The reason for this
must be that he sees himself as two people, one of whom is present
and the other is not. This is the implication of *peece*. He seems
to be saying that only a part of Horatio is actually there on the

ramparts and as he speaks of that Horatio in the third person there is a suggestion that it is not the true Horatio. The true Horatio is still in bed where by implication any sensible person would be on a cold night such as that one is. The presupposition is that he does not want to be where he is; he has been forced against his better judgement to leave his bed and come on what he considers to be a fool's errand. Hence the person present is only a part of Horatio – the body, as it were, but certainly not his logical or reasoning half. He thus distances himself from what is happening and pours cold water on the event. The participants in the conversation clearly know why they have gathered at the watch and what they can expect to see, though we, the audience, do not know yet what the purpose behind this meeting is. We have been led to expect something unusual because of the sense of anticipation which has built up. Horatio's scepticism about the whole purpose of this meeting can only increase the curiosity on the part of the audience and probably bridle the other two participants in the conversation. They do not immediately react to this in so far as Barnardo goes through the pleasantries by welcoming the two newcomers 'Welcome *Horatio*, welcome good *Marcellus*'. He may greet Horatio first because Horatio has just spoken, because he is more senior in status than Marcellus, and perhaps because his apparent scepticism means that he may need to be particularly propitiated by being given precedence. Whether the use of *good* in the address to Marcellus is significant is not clear, but it could be seen as a way of Barnardo responding to what Horatio has just said. Barnardo and Marcellus are already familiar with one another, it implies, and although Horatio may be sceptical the *good* when used of Marcellus suggests that at least he is on the same side as Barnardo. It expresses solidarity. There appears to be a difference between the two arrivals which Barnardo wants to highlight. After all there is no need from the audience's point of view to name these characters because their names have been signposted already in the scene. Their naming is part of the normal process of meeting and part of the means of underlining the difference between them. The contextual situation has turned what is often no more than a conventional epithet into a form of address which has point and meaning.

Marcellus responds to this form of address by showing that he is on Barnardo's side. He says *What ha's this thing appear'd againe to night.* Here we notice immediately that there is a solidarity with Barnardo because there is something which he and Barnardo share. What it is is not explained, but it seems to be something too dangerous to speak of directly. *This thing* is a euphemism to refer to something which cannot be spoken of openly. The fact that it appears may well suggest something supernatural like a ghost. Also its apparent regularity in appearance at night points in the same direction. We, as audience, must assume that the three speakers know what it is, but even so they cannot refer to it directly. The way the conversation has developed enables us to understand why Barnardo had wanted to make sure that Horatio had come and Horatio's scepticism. It is now apparent that the other two share some secret knowledge that they are trying to persuade Horatio to accept, though he is obviously less than enthusiastic about the whole situation. To Marcellus's question Barnardo returns a negative, but instead of simply saying 'No' he breaks the maxim of quantity by saying *I haue seene nothing.* He emphasises the negative he offers, but he also refuses to name what he has not seen. He does not say 'I have not seen the ghost' or something similar, although that is clearly what he means. He has seen something, because he saw Francisco, but he has not seen what they have all come to see, even though he does not want to name it.

By considering the contextual situation we can understand more clearly how some words have a particular meaning and what the presuppositions are which lie behind so many of the utterances. From a stylistic point of view it gives us a greater insight into the language and prompts further lines of enquiry. In this particular case it may be interesting to compare the Folio text with that in the 1603 quarto which may have been based on a memorial reconstruction of the play. This scene is significantly different.

Enter two Centinels
1:     Stand: who is that?
2:     Tis I.
1:     O you come most carefully vpon your watch,
2:     And if you meete *Marcellus* and *Horatio,*
        The partners of my watch, bid them make haste.
1:     I will: See who goes there.

102 AN INTRODUCTION TO THE LANGUAGE OF LITERATURE

Enter Horatio and Marcellus

HOR: Friends to this ground.

MAR: And leegemen to the Dane,
       O farewell honest souldier, who hath releeued you?

1:    *Barnardo* hath my place, giue you good night.

MAR: Holla *Barnardo*.

2:    Say, is *Horatio* there?

HOR: A peece of him.

2:    Welcome *Horatio*, welcome good *Marcellus*.

MAR: What hath this thing appear'd againe to night.

2:    I haue seene nothing.

Although the second half of the passage shows few changes, the first is strikingly different. The characters are not named at first, simply appearing as '1' and '2'. It is the speaker named '1' who opens the conversation, and that turns out to be 'Francisco', though he is never named in this text. He is the sentry on duty and he challenges the newcomer as one would expect a sentry to do. His challenge is not so aggressive as that found in the Folio for it contains the simple imperative *Stand* and the interrogative *who is that?* Barnardo, who is here the '2', simply replies *Tis I* – the reply one might expect at the change of guards. It suggests that the two guards know each other and that the first is expecting the second. The second certainly assumes that the first will know who this '1' is. There is no sense of foreboding or apprehension. The exchange is natural and expected. The first speaker then replies to this identification, which he accepts as sufficient, by noting that '2' has come to take over the watch at the right time. The emphasis on *most carefully* is still there, but does not seem so marked in this context as it has been in the Folio. Certainly '2' does not respond to this comment, which appears to have been made as '1' prepares to leave his position. The remark made now by '2' presupposes the imminent departure of '1' for he asks him to hurry Marcellus and Horatio up if he meets them. Since there has been little to arouse any feeling of hostility or uncertainty in the conversation so far, this request appears to be perfectly natural. The first speaker agrees to this request as he leaves. Neither says good bye to the other, and both seem to be on friendly terms though neither is named. The change of sentries appears to be a routine matter which arouses little apprehension or anxiety on either's part. When Francisco leaves he challenges the two newcomers, though the challenge is somewhat low-key. In modern punctuation it would probably appear as *See, who goes there?* Horatio and Marcellus reply as in the Folio. In this quarto Marcellus gives his answer to the question *who goes there?* and then immediately goes on to say something further. Francisco has no chance to comment on the replies given to his challenge and Marcellus presumably accepts that Francisco would not wish to do so. The result is an exchange which again seems ordinary and routine. Francisco gives the required information and then leaves after saying his good night. The rest of the passage then continues in this quarto much as it was in the Folio. It is by comparing what is in the quarto with the contents of the Folio that one can understand how pragmatics helps us to understand the contextual situation and the presuppositions which lie behind so much of what is said. Naturally such a comparison is not always available, but the earlier analysis of the Folio text itself shows how one can use pragmatics for stylistic information. Through it one can come to a much closer understanding of the language more generally. It is a useful tool which should be exploited much more than is currently the case.

7 Cohesion

Pragmatics, as we have seen, consists of the presuppositions which lie behind utterances which enable us to relate one utterance to the next to form a coherent sequence of meaning within a text. Cohesion is a more visible means of providing the same way of linking utterances together so that they can be seen to belong to a single text. One needs only quote a straightforward example to make this clear. Consider the following two sentences:

7.1 Mrs Jones is coming to tea this afternoon. As she is going to visit the vicar first, she may be a little late.

In the first sentence we are introduced to Mrs Jones. In the second sentence Mrs Jones is referred to twice as *she*. This *she* is a clear reference to Mrs Jones and provides one obvious way in which the second sentence is tied to the first. To that extent the second sentence presupposes the first because it would not be possible to interpret who this *she* is unless the information of the first sentence was already provided. Naturally there are references in this passage which are understood by the speakers themselves, but which may not be clear to anyone else. We do not know who Mrs Jones is; we do not know which afternoon *this afternoon* is; and we do not know who *the* vicar is. These are contextually known to the participants in the conversation. In this chapter we are not so concerned with this contextual information as with the visible ties linking sentences represented by *she* in this instance. It has to be realised that *she*, like other personal pronouns, could in other circumstances be explicable from the contextual situation. If two men are talking in a room and a girl walks past the window, one man might say to the other 'She's a beautiful girl', even though they may not know her name or anything else about her. The context would provide the key to the interpretation of the pronoun.

Cohesion takes place when one element in a text can be interpreted only through another element in the same text, and it is this element of mutuality which helps to create a single text. It is time now to consider some of the ties which can be used to link utterances within a text. From what was noted in the last paragraph, we can divide ties into two major categories: those which are explained through the situation and those which are explained through a tie in the text itself, sometimes referred to respectively as *exophoric* (i.e. situational) and *endophoric* (i.e. textual) references. Endophoric reference can itself be further subdivided into whether the tie looks back to something which is already provided in the text or forward to something which is going to be provided in the text, known respectively as *anaphoric* and *cataphoric* reference. Consider, for example, the following passages:

7.2   Put the potatoes in a saucepan with water and boil them for twenty minutes.
7.3   Putting them in a saucepan with water, boil the potatoes for twenty minutes.

In each sentence *them* occurs and refers to the potatoes. In 7.2 the potatoes occur in the first clause and in the second clause *them* refers back anaphorically to *potatoes*. In 7.3 *them* occurs in the opening phrase and refers forward cataphorically to *potatoes*, which has been delayed until the main clause. Naturally the thing or person referred to may occur at a much greater distance than is true of these two examples, and the tie itself need not be a personal pronoun. Ties normally take one of three forms: personal, demonstrative or comparative. Personal reference is achieved through personal pronouns as well as through possessive adjectives and pronouns. Examples have already been provided in this chapter. Demonstratives include such forms as *this*, *that*, *these* and *those*, and work in much the same way as personal reference. It is possible naturally for a demonstrative to have more than one possible tie to what has gone before or is to come, as in the following examples.

7.4   The student handed in his essay. That was excellent.

In this example the *that* in the second sentence can refer either to the essay itself as being excellent or to the fact that the essay was handed in as being excellent. In many cases the wider context may help to elucidate which of the two is the more likely. Comparative references are expressions of a scale, which can be of similarity, proximity or almost any other feature. Such comparison may be exophoric and take as its point of reference some acknowledged or assumed standard, as in

7.5   You can buy apples more cheaply here.

This sentence presupposes a standard of price elsewhere which is not found in the place advertising apples. The comparison can also be endophoric as in

7.6   The apples are nice, but the pears are tastier.

In this example *tastier* implies 'than the apples', and so it refers anaphorically to *the apples*. It will be appreciated that these forms of tie occur most often within a noun group, acting as subject or complement, though they can also be found in adjuncts.

Another important way of providing cohesive ties is substitution, whereby one linguistic item is replaced by another. This is another way of avoiding repetition in language. Perhaps the most obvious form is when a clause is substituted by a word, as in

7.7   Has the train already gone?
       I think so.

In this example it has to be assumed that *so* is a substitute for the clause *that the train has already gone*, which is not expressed. In this way the second speaker can avoid repeating all that the first speaker has said. A negative reply could be phrased either as 'I don't think so' or 'I think not'. In the first of these, *so* fulfils the same function it had in the positive sentence; in the second, one should probably assume that *not* is a substitute standing for 'that the train has not already left' though few people would express the idea in that way. In both positive and negative forms it may be accepted that *so* and *not* are objects to *think* and thus occupy the same clause function that 'that the train has already left' would fill if it had been expressed. Indeed, in substitution it is common for the substitute to occupy the same function as the item it is acting as substitute for, though in some cases it may embrace more than that single function. In an example like

7.8   Do you know Professor Smith?
        Everyone does.

the *does* stands for 'knows Professor Smith'. Although it functions as predicator, it also in this case functions as the object. The occurrence of a part of the verb *do* signals that some verbal substitution is involved, as in the use of *does* for 'knows' in 7.8.

Substitution can involve a noun, verb or a clause, or perhaps one should say a noun group, verb group or clause. When a noun group is involved the cohesion will be not dissimilar to the type we have just discussed, as in

7.9   Do you see those yellow balls over there?
        The ones on the left?

In this example *the ones* is a substitution for *those yellow balls over there*, which could have as easily been replaced by *those*. Verb substitution through *do*, and clause substitution through *so* or *not* have already been discussed. Substitution is something which is much more closely tied to a text than the previous form of cohesion discussed, and consequently exophoric substitution is rare in this form. If it does occur, it would clearly have to refer to an unsaid sentence, some of which was being substituted in the spoken sentence.

Cohesion through ellipsis is not unlike cohesion through substitution, though in ellipsis there is nothing which is actually substituted for what is said in the previous sentence. All that happens is that some part of the sentence which is needed to complete the sense is omitted, because it can be inferred from what has already been uttered. In an example like

7.10   Those chocolates look scrumptious.
        Let's buy some.

the *some* of the reply cannot be said to substitute for *those chocolates* of the first sentence, since *some* does not refer to all the chocolates, but only to some of them. Hence *some* can reasonably be said to illustrate ellipsis rather than substitution, since it really means 'some of the chocolates'. However, it can be seen from this example that what is missing can readily be supplied by the addressee, and this is true of ellipsis generally. Ellipsis involving the verb normally means that the verb is replaced by an auxiliary, or if the form already contains an auxiliary it is only that which is retained. This can be seen in

7.11   Can you swim?
       Yes, I can.

Here the *can* of the reply is an elliptical form for *can swim*. However, when this type of verbal ellipsis takes place, it will more often involve the complement as well as the lexical part of the verb, as in

7.12   Do you like swimming?
       Yes, I do.

Here the *do* stands for *do like swimming* and not just for *do like*. Less frequently there may be ellipsis of the subject as well as the verb, but when that happens the verb will leave no trace, not even the auxiliary. Such constructions are somewhat literary, as in

7.13   The dog barks at the cat in the house and at the pheasants on his walks.

This sentence could be said to consist of two clauses: *the dog barks at the cat in the house*, and *the dog barks at the pheasants on his walks*. The two are collapsed by omitting the second *the dog barks*, and this omission is understood as an example of ellipsis. Ellipsis of a clause is also quite common. Substitution is when a clause is replaced by a word like *so*; ellipsis happens when no word is introduced as a substitute. Consider the following example, which can be compared with 7.7

7.14   Has the train already gone?
       I don't know.

In 7.14 the complement clause *whether the train has already gone* is omitted entirely and so the sentence constitutes an example of ellipsis. In 7.7 the answer to the question had been *I think so*, where *so* was a substitute for the complement clause *that the train has already gone*. Verbs which are transitive and require a complement may not have the complement expressed, if it can be inferred from the rest of the text.

Cohesion can be expressed through less obvious means than those already noted. Language proceeds sequentially and there is a natural assumption that there is a temporal or causal relationship between two utterances when one follows immediately after the other. At least this will be the case if the two utterances can be thought to have some relationship, unlike the two sentences which were quoted at the beginning of the chapter. So in a passage like

7.15   The director got very angry. He banged his fist on the table and swore at his staff.

it will be assumed, correctly enough, that there is a direct relationship between the fact of the director getting angry and the actions of banging the table and swearing. The temporal relationship is such that we accept that the getting angry preceded the other two actions. It would seem distinctly odd if the passage read:

7.15a The director banged his fist on the table and swore at his staff. He got very angry.

Since we tend to assume that banging a table and swearing are a result of anger rather than its cause, we would expect the fact of getting angry to come first. Sentence 7.15a is by no means impossible, but it does imply that the actions took place in a sequence which we would not have expected. It would not be possible to interpret 7.15a as though anger preceded the other actions.

Because *got* is a dynamic verb, we attach a time sequence to it. This would not be true of stative verb forms like *is* or *was*. If 7.15a had as its second sentence *He was very angry*, there would be no difficulty because the stative nature of the verb would be regarded as operative during the actions of the first sentence. The relationship between two sentences may be causal rather than temporal, though in modern written English causality is normally expressed through a conjunction. In older varieties of English and in colloquial English this is not so, and this often presents problems of punctuation at a written level. A sentence like

7.16 Watch out, he's coming.

would probably be unacceptable to many people at the written level because they would expect each clause to be a separate sentence. There is clearly a relationship between the two clauses, which in more formal English might have to be expressed something like *Because he's coming, take care*. That the more colloquial arrangement was widely used in earlier forms of English is shown by an example in the *The Merchant of Venice*: 'The Hebrew will turne Christian, he growes kinde' (I.iii.173).

Naturally it is possible to rearrange many of the sentences we have been discussing so that they form a single sentence. This can be done through the use of conjunctions or through the use of phrases or nominalisation. The example in 7.15 could be rewritten in the following ways, even if they do not all mean quite the same thing:

7.15b Getting angry, the director banged his fist on the table and swore at his staff.

7.15c When he got angry, the director banged his fist on the table and swore at his staff.

7.15d Because he got angry, the director banged his fist on the table and swore at his staff.

7.15e After he got angry, the director banged his fist on the table and swore at his staff.

The sentences in 7.15b–e do not mean the same thing because they are all more fully specified than 7.15 itself. It could be said that the advantage of 7.15 is precisely that it can imply so many of the meanings in the other sentences. In poetry the juxtaposition of sentences without stating their relationship, but only inferring it, is one way in which multiple meaning can be suggested.

It is possible to weld a text together through the choice of lexis. In some ways this can at one end be not far removed from the use of a pronoun for a noun. When, for example, one uses a more general word to designate the type or class to which the more specific word belongs, one is behaving in much the same way as using a pronoun for a noun. The *flower* of one sentence could be referred to as the *daffodil* in the next. The change is from a more general to a more specific referent. Naturally it is possible to use words which have the same referent but which do not occupy a place in a hierarchical order; the words may be variants, though one may well be more marked than the other. In a sentence like

7.17   Suddenly the animal woke up. The beast started to come towards me.

animal and *beast* are understood to be interchangeable lexical items. It may well be that *beast* has slightly more terrifying connotations than *animal* which is more neutral, but denotatively they are not too far apart. Equally they do not exist in a hierarchical relationship, because a beast is not a subset of animal any more than animal is a subset of beast.

The previous example does raise the interesting problem of metaphor, since a lexical item can be replaced by another on a metaphorical rather than on a literal level of meaning. If one were to rewrite 7.17 as

7.17a Suddenly the man woke up. The beast started to come towards me.

one would understand *beast* as being another way of saying *man*, since it would clearly be impossible for *man* to be a lexical tie for *me*. Naturally within literary works this type of lexical variation appears as a tie. Consider, for example, the following passage from *King Lear*:

ALBANY: See thy selfe deuill,
             Proper deformity shewes not in the fiend
             So horid as in woman.
GONERIL: O vaine fool!
ALBANY: Thou changed, and selfe-couerd thing for shame
             Be-monster not thy feature, wer't my fitnes
             To let these hands obay my bloud,

They are apt enough to dislocate and teare
Thy flesh and bones, how ere thou art a fiend
A womans shape doth shield thee.

(IV.ii.59–67)

Here one can see certain words which lexically relate to each
other such as *deuill*, *fiend* and *monster*, though these words
are both contrasted with and regarded as equivalent to *woman*.
Equally there is another group of words which belong to the same
semantic field: *deformity*, *changed*, *selfe-couerd* (in the sense that
it is not in the proper shape it should be), *be-monster*, *dislocate* and
teare, since all these words suggest the sense of being abnormal
in appearance in some way, particularly in a way which is non-
human and frightening. Another group of words relate to what
might be considered natural in humans, words such as *woman*,
feature, *bloud*, *flesh*, *bones* and *shape*. Many of these words are
set in contrast to what is unnatural and changed from the human.
In this short passage the words indicating change in some form
indicate that the words indicating humanity on the one hand and
the supernatural on the other, which ought to be kept apart, have
in fact been linked so that there is a progression from woman to
fiend. In this way there is a very close link between the various
lexical items which appear in the passage.

Lexical cohesion can operate through the repetition of the
same idea but using a different word, such as *fiend* and *deuill*. It
can operate through contrast such as *woman* and *fiend*, because
one is human and the other supernatural. It can operate through
collocation, where words that are often found together also occur
in the passage. In *King Lear* we notice that *flesh* and *bloud* occur
in this passage, though they do not occur as a doublet *flesh and
bloud*. The two words are separated by a couple of lines and
flesh occurs as a doublet with *bones*. Such a doublet is obvious
enough since these two items are the most prominent features
of human beings in their physical shape, for the doublet *flesh
and bloud* is more often used in a slightly more abstract sense
meaning 'humanity'. In this passage the emphasis is rather on
the physical quality of human beings. There are words which
can be said to have lexical ties in this passage even at a more
abstract level. *Proper* and *fitnes* belong together and may be said
to contrast with *shame*. *Fool* could be said to be another word for

man in this context (as it refers to Albany) and as such it appears to contrast with *woman* and *fiend*. *Fool* carries with it the sense of naive innocence as compared with the wickedness of the dev- ilish woman. *Couerd* (i.e. covered) has a lexical link with *shield*, since a shield covers the body. A body which is falsely covered as Goneril's appears to be, because a woman's shape conceals a devil beneath, is contrasted with a shield, which would normally be used to protect a man's body from harm at a physical level.

In poetry cohesion can also be thought of as the means of internal patterning such as stanza, refrain, rhyme, alliteration and related techniques. Linguistic cohesion, as we have seen, refers rather to the patterns within the language elements, and this can be at any level: sentence, clause, word or even morpheme. No doubt the better poems will contain cohesion at many levels, but will not make it too obvious. Too much surface cohesion will seem too pat and may well make the reader think that the poem is no more than verse doggerel. However, enough has now been said about the general principle of cohesion and it is time to test it against the two passages we have been using in the rest of this book, Sonnet 129 and *Mansfield Park*. I shall begin by considering the Shakespearian sonnet, and it may be appropriate to quote it in full again:

1 TH'expence of Spirit in a waste of shame
2 Is lust in action, and till action, lust
3 Is periurd, murdrous, blouddy full of blame,
4 Sauage, extreame, rude, cruell, not to trust,
5 Inioyd no sooner but dispised straight,
6 Past reason hunted, and no sooner had
7 Past reason hated as a swollowed bayt,
8 On purpose layd to make the taker mad.
9 Mad In pursut and in possession so,
10 Had, hauing, and in quest to haue extreame,
11 A blisse in proofe and proud and very wo,
12 Before a ioy proposd behind a dreame,
13 All this the world well knowes yet none knowes well,
14 To shun the heauen that leads men to this hell.

As we have seen earlier in this book, this sonnet has the cohesive features of most sonnets. It consists of fourteen lines rhyming ababcdcdefefgg, and this provides a very tight pattern organi-sationally. The same is true of the metre and sound patterns. These features have been sufficiently examined earlier not to need further elaboration here. This sonnet is unusual in that it has very few endophoric references, because there are few pronominal forms. In part this is because there are almost no human agents in this sonnet, or at least none which are referred to directly as agents. Many of the subjects are abstract or generalised. There is reference to *the taker* (8) and to *men* (14), but these references are themselves non-specific. *Taker* is presumably anyone who takes the bait which has been laid rather than a specific person, and *men* refers to all those who indulge in lust as described in the rest of the sonnet. *Taker* and *men* are respectively a specific example of what is more general, though neither is personalised. The two do stand in a cohesive relation to each other, just as *the world* and *none* do. They stand for everybody and nobody, but are themselves non-specific.

Because there are no human agents, it is hardly surprising that there are no personal pronouns. There are two examples of *this* (13 and 14). The first in the expression *All this* refers back to everything that has been enumerated in lines 9–12 and indeed more generally to the whole of what precedes in the sonnet. *All* stands in a contrastive cohesive relation with *none*. The second *this* occurs in the phrase *this hell*, and this other *this* also refers to all that has gone before in the sonnet in so far as this hell implies all the misfortune which has been so graphically described from a *waste of shame* right through till *very wo*. It is natural that a couplet at the end of a sonnet should both recapitulate and summarise what has gone before, and so the occurrence of *this* twice provides the tie which links the couplet back to the ideas introduced earlier. At a different level it could be said that *hell* has a cohesive tie with *expence* at the beginning of the sonnet since the price one pays for all that one enjoys in lust is hell; what you buy with this expenditure is hell.

Because there are few pronominal forms, cohesion in this sonnet takes the form of lexical tie either through parallelism or through contrast, though it could be said that there are also lexical cohesive sets formed through series. Even thematically there could be said to be cohesion in so far as the poem appears to describe lust in action, but it underscores that the reward of lust in action is self-deception and misery. Hence there is a link between hunting and fishing in lines 6–8. Both are sports where man goes in pursuit of a quarry, but the two run into each other. The hunter catches only himself because the bait he lays out for others is the bait he gets hooked on. This theme is parallel to that in the conclusion of the sonnet since man goes out in pursuit of heaven, but he finds only hell.

There are some lexical ties which consist of the repetition of the same words and these fall into two categories. The first category contains repetition almost immediately and helps to create parallels across clauses or phrases. Both *lust* and *action* occur twice in line 2 and provide the cohesion between the two clauses of the first sentence. *No sooner* and *past reason* occur twice each over lines 5–7 and thus help to provide the parallelism between the series of phrases which occur in these lines. *Well knowes* occurs twice in line 13 and this provides the cohesion between the final two clauses of the sonnet, and in turn this link is parallel to the first tie in the sonnet. Each clause in each sentence is tied by lexical means to provide a taut structure overall. The second category contains repetition over a longer stretch of the sonnet, usually indeed between the first and the second sentence. *Extreame* occurs in lines 4 and 10; *had* in lines 6 and 10; *mad* in lines 8 and 9; and *inioyd* in line 5 is repeated as *ioy* in line 12. Naturally some lexical items stand in a contrastive lexical relationship, though this is more characteristic of the second half than of the first. The first half exhibits progression rather than straight contrast, though in line 5 it could be said that *inioyd* and *dispised* do exhibit a contrast. In the second half the final lines are all built on some kind of lexical contrast: *blisse* and *wo*, *ioy* and *dreame*, *the world* and *none*, and *heaven* and *hell*. Some of these words stand in the same semantic field such as *blisse*, *ioy* and *heauen* and so provide a different range of lexical ties, but this is to anticipate what we must now consider.

There are several areas of meaning which consist of words in the same semantic fields, and these also provide cohesion within each sentence as well as across the two sentences. Consider the word *action*, which occurs twice in line 2. Gradually it becomes clear that this word introduces a range of words implying activity, which in this sonnet are related to hunting and associated sports. In line 3 the words *murdrous* and *blouddy* are found, neither of which seem appropriate to a portrayal of lust. But they are part of the semantic field of hunting, which leads to the bloody murder of the animals which are hunted as part of the action. Hunting may be said to be *sauage, rude* (i.e. barbaric) and *cruell* (4) because it means the pursuit of the animal leading to its death and the animal may not be able to defend itself in any serious way. This leads on to the word *hunted* (6), which we assume to relate to hunting in the field for animals such as the deer or the fox. In line 7 *bayt* is specific to fishing, which is another form of hunting activity, though fishing itself is not mentioned. Although some kinds of trapping might involve the use of bait, it is only in fishing where one might think specifically that the bait is swallowed. The bait is *layd* (8) out for the fish and when the fish takes (cf *taker*) the bait it thrashes around in the water as though it is frenzied or *mad* (8), which can therefore be said to be within this semantic field. This web of words is continued in the second sentence because hunting involves *pursut* (9) and ultimately *possession* of the prize (9) whether that should be an animal or a fish. Hunting also involves a *quest* (10) since one has to seek out the animal before one can actually hunt it. The quest to find the animal is said to be *extreame* (10) just as the concept of lust as hunting was *extreame* in the first sentence (4).

The semantic field outlined in the last paragraph is the main one in the sonnet and provides the major conceptual framework since it contains the metaphorical equation of sexual pleasure with hunting, an equation which was common enough at that time and has remained so. Traditionally the male is portrayed as a hunter in pursuit of the female, though neither sex is specifically referred to since the poem works by suggestion rather than by direct statement. Other ties exist, but do not extend so far. *Expence* is linked to *waste*, since the cost of something is closely related to whether one uses it wisely or wastes it. *Expence*, as suggested already, is related to the cost of the hunting and it is seen to be a bad bargain. The *expence* incurred is seen to be a *waste* since it leads to *hell*. This range of meaning is set against words like *spirit*, which imply something more spiritual than physical. Lust is a physical action that misdirects the human spirit and leads to its waste. *Spirit* is linked to *trust* (the absence of which is deplored), *inioyed, reason, blisse, ioy* and *heauen*. These words do not occur as often as those for the activity of the hunt, but they occur often enough to remind the reader of the alternative way of life. *Shame*, which comes from the refusal to employ the spirit properly, is linked to *periurd*, *blame*, *not to trust* (i.e. untrustworthy), *dispised*, *hated*, *mad*, *wo* and *hell*, since these are all words which have unfavourable connotations attached to them and are usually associated with people that come in for disapproval. These words are also related to *past reason*, i.e. beyond what is reasonable. The realm of the spirit is that which observes the dictates of reason; the flesh goes beyond reason and in a mad state undertakes actions which are shameful and blameworthy. People who behave in this way perjure themselves and cannot be trusted. These words are in themselves not too far away from those expressing immediacy in the time scale, such as *no sooner* and *straight*. Those who are mad in lust want immediate gratification, and this sense of immediacy is implied, though not stated, in the final line. This activity leads to hell and that is inevitable as well as immediate because lust is no sooner had than the object of it is hated, which is one form of hell.

Cohesion takes place in a different way from the purely lexical in that the sonnet consists of certain concepts which are little more than different ways of saying the same thing. The cohesion comes from this repetition of a basic idea in a variety of different words and grammatical ways. Lines 3 and 4 contain a sequence of words. All these words have bad connotations, but they have different semantic fields. As we have seen *periurd* goes with *shame*, but *murdrous* and *blouddy* with hunting. By putting these words in the same series, there is the implication that all these unfavourable connotations are intimately linked. But this list represents a series which is part of a wider series expressed over the following lines; the similarity of treatment acts as a cohesive feature in the poem as a whole. In these lines there is also a morphemic cohesion, since so many of the words in them end with the inflexional ending *-(e)d*: *periurd, inioyd, dispised, hunted, had, hated, swollowed* and *layd*. This echo of the *-(e)d* ending ties these words and phrases together closely.

Some of these types of cohesion are less likely to be found in prose which is not arranged in metrical or even rhythmical units, and in which one does not expect to find too much verbal or morphemic echo lest the prose should be considered too overwrought. In earlier periods of English prose was rather closer to poetry in this type of cohesion, but more recently it has become more fashionable to be less elaborate. Cohesion is more subdued than in the poetry, and this can be seen in the opening of *Mansfield Park*:

(1) About thirty years ago, Miss Maria Ward of Huntingdon, with only seven thousand pounds, had the good luck to captivate Sir Thomas Bertram, of Mansfield Park, in the county of Northampton, and to be thereby raised to the rank of a baronet's lady, with all the comforts and consequences of an handsome house and large income. (2) All Huntingdon exclaimed on the greatness of the match, and her uncle, the lawyer, himself, allowed her to be at least three thousand pounds short of any equitable claim to it. (3) She had two sisters to be benefited by her elevation; and such of their acquaintance as thought Miss Ward and Miss Frances quite as handsome as Miss Maria, did not scruple to predict their marrying with almost equal advantage. (4) But there certainly are not so many men of large fortune in the world, as there are pretty women to deserve them. (5) Miss Ward, at the end of half a dozen years, found herself obliged to be attached to the Rev. Mr Norris, a friend of her brother-in-law, with scarcely any private fortune, and Miss Frances fared yet worse. (6) Miss Ward's match, indeed, when it came to the point, was not contemptible, Sir Thomas being happily able to give his friend an income in the living of Mansfield, and Mr and Mrs Norris began their career of conjugal felicity with very little less than a thousand a year.

As one might expect in prose there are more pronominal forms acting as ties across sentences. In sentence 1 we are introduced to *Miss Maria Ward* and *Sir Thomas Bertram*. In sentence 2 both examples of *her* refer back to *Miss Maria Ward*. In sentence 3 the opening *she* refers to her as well, but later in the sentence she is referred to as *Miss Maria*, rather than as Lady Bertram, because it is her potential as a marriage partner which is at issue. In this sentence *Miss Maria* is said to have *two sisters* and as these now become the focus of attention, she drops out of the picture and there are no further references to her. The *their* of *their marrying* refers to these other sisters. In sentence 4 *them* links back to *men of large fortune* earlier in the sentence. In sentence 5 *herself* and *her* refer to *Miss Ward*, who is here linked with *Mr Norris*, who is said to be *a friend of her brother-in-law*, i.e. Sir Thomas Bertram. The brother-in-law is linked cohesively with the two sisters of sentence 3. In sentence 6 *Sir Thomas* is referred to by name and so *his friend* now means Mr Norris, and *their career* refers to that of Mr and Mrs Norris.

The major theme of this passage is marriage, particularly as it concerns these three sisters. Marriage is mentioned or implied in every sentence, though there is no reference to a wedding or marriage ceremony. In sentence 1 Miss Maria Ward is said to *captivate* Sir Thomas and *to be thereby raised* to the rank of a baronet's lady; in sentence 4 Miss Ward *found herself obliged to be attached* to the Rev. Mr Norris, and Miss Frances *fared yet worse*. The marriages are seen in terms of social class and advantage, which are largely pecuniary. Here there is a clear pecking order: one sister does very well; another sister does moderately well; and the youngest does very badly – at least as far as the social and financial aims of marriage are concerned. There is cohesion in these what might almost be called non-references to marriage, because of the roundabout way in which it is addressed, and also in the declining graph of successfulness of the three sisters. There are, however, many other references to marriage and match-making in the passage. In sentence 2 there is reference to the *match*, i.e. the marriage of Miss Maria and Sir Thomas, and in sentence 6 there is reference to *Miss Ward's match*, i.e. her marriage to the Rev. Mr Norris. In sentence 3 there is reference to the *elevation* of Miss Maria, i.e. her rise in the social scale through her marriage to Sir Thomas, and there is also mention of the enhanced prospects of the other two *marrying with almost equal advantage*, i.e. marrying people who are socially and financially superior to them. In sentence 4 there is mention of the pretty women who *deserve* men of large fortune, and by *deserve* is meant that they should marry them to their advantage. Finally in sentence 6 there is the expression *conjugal felicity*, which refers to the married state, if not specifically to marriage as such. All these references to marriage help to provide cohesion within the passage.

Money and social advancement are also very much involved as themes in this opening paragraph of the novel. This is first introduced by *raised* and confirmed by *the comforts and consequences of an handsome house and large income*. In the first sentence Miss Maria's own inheritance of *only seven thousand pounds* raises the question of money as an element in marriage directly. This is continued in the next sentence, where it is said that she was *three thousand pounds short of any equitable claim* to the match she had won for herself. In sentence 3 the importance of money in marriage is stressed through the references to *elevation* and *equal advantage*. In the following sentence we are introduced to *men of large fortune*. In sentence 5 poor Mr Norris is said to have *scarcely any private fortune*, and as Miss Frances *fared yet worse* it can mean only that she married a husband with no private income at all. In the sixth sentence the income of the newly married Norrises is put at *very little less than a thousand a year*. Money is referred to in every sentence either directly or indirectly, usually the former. It is interesting that there is such a strong cohesive tie formed by words like *thousand* (pounds) and *fortune* in which the focus on cash is quite unambiguous, whereas the act of marrying itself is referred to by circumlocutions. Cohesion is expressed strongly through the financial side of marriage. There is little emphasis and hence only weak cohesion on the qualities the sisters might bring to marriage. Since Miss Maria can *captivate* Sir Thomas, there is an implication that she is beautiful and intelligent enough to do so. In sentence 3 the two sisters are said to be *quite as handsome as Miss Maria* and hence a scale is established. Since we do not know how handsome Miss Maria is, it is difficult to decide how attractive the other sisters are too. It is also significant that *handsome* is a word used also of the house which Miss Maria occupies through her marriage, and this cohesive tie suggests that the sisters are marketable property whose value has to be exploited. In sentence 4 there is reference to *pretty women*, which by implication the three sisters are. The fate of the three sisters exemplifies the dictum promulgated in this sentence, because only one of the three can find a man of large fortune. The cohesive links among expressions of female excellence are far fewer than those which pinpoint money and social class. It might also be said that the references to women all suggest that they may have beauty but that they are financially less secure. At least their object in life is understood to be to use their talents to increase their financial and social position. Beauty and wealth do not necessarily go hand in hand.

In the opening sentence there is an example of contrastive cohesion between *Miss Maria Ward of Huntingdon* and *Sir Thomas Bertram, of Mansfield Park, in the county of Northampton*. This contrast is an implicit social one. Miss Ward is clearly not socially elevated because she has no title other than *Miss*, which is available to all unmarried women. She is also said to be *of Huntingdon*. This could be either the town or the county, but the former is surely correct. Sir Thomas not only is a baronet but also has a seat, *Mansfield Park*. That is located in a county. Sir Thomas is a landed man of wealth, though his fortune is implied rather than stated. Miss Maria Ward is from a town and has an income of seven thousand pounds but no social position. There is a contrast of sex, social position and wealth. There is also the implied contrast of beauty as compared with landed property; for Sir Thomas has no need to be intelligent or handsome since he has the position which is sufficient recommendation as a husband. This social contrast is implied in the second sentence since Miss Maria Ward has an uncle who is a lawyer. To have a professional man rather than a member of the landed class as an uncle marks her out as someone who comes from the middle or professional classes. There is a cohesion in references to the three sisters, but that is also one of scale. Only one sister is referred to by her full name, *Miss Maria Ward*. Another sister is called *Miss Ward* and later *Mrs Norris*, whereas the third is called simply *Miss Frances*. Neither of these two sisters has the additional title *of Huntingdon*, because they are clearly poorer in every way.

In ways such as those outlined above we can trace the ties which link the various sentences together in a text and, perhaps just as importantly, provide us with insights as to what is important in them. It is through providing such ties that authors can build up what they think important as a motif in their work. Cohesion helps us to understand the overall structure of a work more completely.

8 Conclusion

In the chapters in this book so far we have considered the various linguistic mechanisms that can be examined as part of the stylistic analysis of a literary text. It is time now to consider all these mechanisms together within the framework of a particular poem so that their interrelationship can be understood. In the previous chapters I have looked at Shakespeare's Sonnet 129 and Jane Austen's *Mansfield Park*. So it will be appropriate in this chapter to analyse a more modern text and I have chosen for this purpose W. H. Auden's short lyric 'This Lunar Beauty', which was written in April 1930. To start with let us quote the entire poem:

This Lunar Beauty

1 This lunar beauty
2 Has no history,
3 Is complete and early;
4 If beauty later
5 Bear any feature,
6 It had a lover
7 And is another.

8 This like a dream
9 Keeps other time,
10 And daytime is
11 The loss of this;
12 For time is inches
13 And the heart's changes,
14 Where ghost has haunted
15 Lost and wanted.

16 But this was never
17 A ghost's endeavour
18 Nor, finished this,
19 Was ghost at ease;
20 And till it pass
21 Love shall not near
22 The sweetness here,
23 Nor sorrow take
24 His endless look.

In the light of the earlier chapters it is possible to think of a poem stylistically from two major points of view: within the sentence or beyond the sentence. As a general principle it is probably easier to start with the grammar within the sentence, though some aspects such as rhyme and stanza pattern may form a suitable starting-point. Within a sentence there are different features which have formed the basis of individual chapters in the first half of the book. It is possible to start by tackling any of these features, the overall structure, the noun group, the other groups, vocabulary or rhetoric. Unless there are particular aspects of the poem which strike one on first reading that appear to demand immediate attention, it will usually be most informative to start with the overall structure, which will in any case fit in with the consideration of stanza and rhyme patterns. In 'This Lunar Beauty' there are three stanzas, each of which is end-stopped and so apparently forms a syntactic unity by itself. The stanzas are not identical, for the first has seven lines, the second eight, and the final one nine. There appears to be some progression or at least increase in weight with every stanza. Each stanza appears to fall into two halves, because there is a semi-colon at the end of line 3 in the first stanza and at the end of lines 11 and 19 in the other two stanzas. One would therefore expect the stanzas to contain two major clauses separated by the semi-colon. In addition each half of each stanza appears to have a further subdivision indicated by a comma at the end of some lines. In the first stanza a comma at the end of line 2 suggests the first clause falls into two parts of two lines and one line respectively. The comma at the end of line 5 breaks the second clause into two two-line units. In the second stanza there are commas at the end of lines 9 and 13 suggesting that each half-stanza is further broken down into two-line units. The third stanza

is different because the comma at the end of line 18 is matched
with the comma earlier in the line to set off the non-finite clause
finished this. There is no break indicated by punctuation in this
half-stanza. The second half-stanza has a break indicated by the
comma at the end of line 22. That comma is followed in line 23 by
a *Nor* which is also the first word of line 18, where one would have
expected the second part of the first half-stanza to begin.

Apart from looking at what information the punctuation provides us with – information which is less helpful in the case of
Shakespeare's sonnet because the Elizabethans used punctuation
in a different way from that found in modern English – we need
to consider the information provided by the rhyming sequence.
Rhyme may not be the most appropriate word to use since Auden
does not for the most part use true rhymes; he employs assonance
and feminine rhyme in which only the inflexional ending rhymes.
In the first stanza there are two rhymes, one for each half-stanza.
The first three lines have the feminine rhyme in -*y* and the next
four lines have a rhyme in -*er*/-*ure*. The rhymes do not follow the
further subdivision of the two half-stanzas, and the fact that -*er*
and -*ure* are not pure rhymes is immaterial for the rhymes are
suggestive rather than dominant. In the second stanza the rhymes
fall into a couplet pattern of aabbccdd so that the rhymes echo
the division not only of half-stanzas but also of the subdivision
of those half-stanzas into couplets. In the first couplet there is
consonance only on /m/ and in the second couplet assonance on
/i/. The second half-stanza has two feminine rhymes based on
inflexional endings. The third stanza breaks this pattern, which
might have been expected because of its nine lines. The rhyming
pattern is aabbbccdd, a pattern which is at odds with the structural
organisation suggested by the punctuation. The first couplet has
a rhyme extending over two syllables, for the -*ever* of *never* and
the -*eavour* of *endeavour* constitute a pure rhyme, for the sounds
are identical despite the differences in spelling. Although, as we
have seen, there is no punctuation to suggest a syntactic break
after *endeavour*, the rhyme suggests that the couplet could form
a syntactic unit. The next three lines (18–20) could be said to
rhyme together since *this* and *pass* exhibit consonance on /s/, but
ease although written with an [s] actually has the sound /z/ as its
final consonant. But there is little doubt that these three words are
supposed to form a rhyming triad. However, this rhyme sequence

spills across the structural and syntactic organisation since the first two lines belong to the first half-stanza and the third line to the second half-stanza. At present we must think of it as a means of linking these two half-stanzas together more closely than is done in the other stanzas. Lines 21 and 22, like lines 16 and 17, have a pure rhyme despite the difference in spelling, but lines 23 and 24 revert to assonance, this time on /k/. This is the only rhyme or assonance to use one of the so-called hard consonants and it provides a firm ending for the poem. Equally the fact that this last couplet has rhymes on /k/ in monosyllables suggests a stronger conclusion than would have been true of the feminine rhymes which rely on inflexional endings in bisyllabic or even trisyllabic words. This last stanza is quite different from the other stanzas in having two pure rhymes, a rhyme which extends over the syntactic structure of the two half-stanzas, and a final consonance built on the sound /k/. All of this provides useful information which we need to keep in mind as we move towards a more linguistic analysis of the poem.

As we have seen the punctuation suggests that each stanza contains a sense unit, and that each is further subdivided into smaller units. These we must now consider from the syntactical structure, since a preliminary consideration of the poem suggests that its structure rather than its vocabulary will cause problems for most readers. The first stanza is divided into two units by the semi-colon at the end of line 3, but there are commas at the end of lines 2 and 5. Lines 1–3 contain two predicators, *Has* and *Is*, but there appears to be only a single subject, namely *This lunar beauty* in the first line. Hence the reader naturally makes the assumption that this subject serves for both predicators to provide a syntactic organisation SPO, PC, which could also be expressed as SPO(S)PC. In the first clause the predicator takes an object, *no history*, but in the second one the predicator takes a complement, *complete and early*, which is itself made up of two adjectives linked by *and*. In the second half of the stanza there is a comma at the end of line 5, though this serves to mark off a subordinate clause which is here acting as an adjunct. However, the last two lines do contain two predicators, *had* and *is*, and it is perhaps no coincidence that they come from the same two verbs found in the predicators in lines 2 and 3. However, these two predicators are not separated by a comma, since the two clauses which contain them are linked by *And*, unlike the two in the first half of the stanza. The second of the two predicators has no subject expressed, and so we assume that the subject of the first clause, namely *It*, is carried over to the second. This produces the syntactic pattern SPOandPC, which could be expressed alternatively as SPOand(S)PC, which apart from the inclusion of *and* is identical with the pattern in the first half of the stanza. Or rather it is without the inclusion of the adjunct, for the pattern is actually ASPOandPC. The adjunct acts as a kind of fulcrum around which two identical syntactic structures balance against each other.

In the second stanza there is a semi-colon at the end of line 11 and commas at the end of lines 9 and 13. In lines 8–12 there are two predicators, *keeps* and *is*, and each has a subject, *This* and *daytime*. We probably have to interpret *like a dream* as an adjunct, since it can be moved around the clause easily enough to other positions. The result is the following pattern SAPOandSPC. We can see some similarity already with the structure of the first stanza. Each contains few clause elements and there is a single adjunct, though its position is different. In the two clauses there is one dynamic verb with an object and one stative verb with a complement. The second half of this stanza is rather more difficult to analyse. The opening word provides the first problem since *For* is most often a conjunction introducing a subordinate clause, though it can also function as an adjunct but it does so only in a style which is relatively informal. Lines 12 and 13 contain a single predicator, *is*. The occurrence of *And* at the beginning of line 13 suggests that the noun group in that line must be linked co-ordinately with one of the noun groups in line 12 and the most natural one to link it to would be *inches* which acts as the complement to *is*. Consequently these lines have the syntactic structure for SPC, though the complement, like that in line 3, consists of two co-ordinated parts, *inches* and *the heart's changes*. If *For* is interpreted as an adjunct, the structure would be ASPC. The second half of this part of the stanza is equally problematical as far as structure is concerned. It opens with *Where* at the beginning of line 14, which is also normally a relative which introduces a subordinate clause. Perhaps on the analogy with *For* it might be understood as an adjunct, though this seems unlikely. The subject of the clause appears to be *ghost* and its predicator is *has haunted*. This verb, when it has an animate subject and an auxiliary formed from *to have* rather than from *to be*, is normally transitive, though it may be used in a figurative sense. It would therefore usually be followed by an object. It is this role which one might expect *Where* to occupy, though it does not normally fulfil that function. When it acts in an absolute or relative capacity, it normally has the function of an adjunct meaning something like 'in the place where'. It occurs with intransitive verbs or with transitive verbs which have an object: *where he lived, where he built a town.* The problems of this clause are further increased by line 15, *Lost and wanted.* The echo of the three past participles, *haunted, lost, wanted,* suggests that they all fulfil the same syntactic function, in this case that they are all dependent upon the auxiliary *has.* If so, one might have expected a comma after *haunted.* Alternatively *Lost* and *wanted* could be past participles acting as adjectives which might be describing *ghost,* as though it meant that the ghost, lost and wanted, has haunted. Naturally it is possible to assume that *Lost* and *wanted* may actually refer back in this way not to *ghost,* but to *the heart's changes.* This could be so either in the function of participial adjective or even as the past participle of a predicator with the auxiliary understood *(are) lost and wanted.* These latter possibilities are less convincing, and it therefore seems right to assume that *Lost* and *wanted* are part of the final clause even though their precise syntactic function is far from clear. This second half of the second stanza is complicated syntactically. One assumes that there must be a main clause and so it seems best to interpret *For* as an adjunct in line 12 to allow the first clause to operate as a main clause. This makes it different from the *If* in line 4 which introduces the second half of the first stanza, for that is a subordinating conjunction and not an adjunct. If the clause beginning with *Where* at the start of line 14 is interpreted as a subordinate one, the second half of this stanza contrasts with the second half of the first stanza in having a clause acting as adjunct at its end rather than at its beginning. This second stanza is not easy to analyse syntactically, but the range of possibilities has been explored.

In the third stanza there is a semi-colon at the end of line 19. There is no comma at the end of line 17 though *Nor* begins the next line, but there is a comma at the end of line 22 and *Nor* begins lines 23. We have at least two major clauses separated by the semi-colon and we must take each half-stanza as a unit. The stanza opens with the conjunction *But* used as an adjunct. There follow two predicators, both *was*, to provide us with two clauses. The first has *this* as its subject and the second *ghost*. Lines 16–17 have a sentence consisting of ASPnegC, where *neg* stands for 'negator', in this case *never*. The two clauses are linked by *Nor* which co-ordinates two main clauses together in this case and provides a negator as well. The phrase *finished this* has to be understood as an adjunct, meaning something like 'when or after this was finished'. This adjunct is then followed by the predicator and subject in inverse order, an order which is traditionally associated with the appearance of an adjunct as the first clause element. The pattern of the second clause in this first half is therefore negAPSA. The second half-stanza opens with the conjunction *And*. Like the *But* at the beginning of the stanza this might best be understood to be operating as an adjunct, perhaps with the sense of 'indeed, furthermore'. This is followed by *till* which introduces a subordinate clause with the predicator *pass*, so that *till it pass* acts as an adjunct of time. The next line contains the subject *Love* and the verb *shall near*, consisting of an auxiliary and head, together with the negator *not*. The organisation of lines 20–22 might be described as AASauxnegPOA. In fact the last two lines are linked closely with these three because the auxiliary *shall* also governs the predicator *take* in line 23. This line opens with the negator *Nor*, which joins the two clauses together, for although *shall* refers to both *near* and *take* these are still two separate clauses. Each has a subject, *Love* and *sorrow*, and each has a predicator *shall near* and (*shall*) *take*. The pattern of the last two lines is negSPO.

Even before we try to take account of the meaning, there are significant patterns which recur in this poem and which can be said to help to provide some of its cohesion. The poem opens with an SPO structure and it concludes with another SPO structure. The latter one has a negator outside the main structure whereas the opening one has a negator as part of its object *no history*. The opening half-stanza consists of two clauses which share a common subject, whereas the closing half-stanza consists of two stanzas which share a common auxiliary. In the final stanza each half-stanza opens with a conjunction acting as an adjunct, and this seems to be true of the last half-stanza of the second stanza. The final half of the poem commences its half-stanzas in a different way from those found in its first half. The first and the final stanzas commence their second half-stanza with a subordinate clause acting as an adjunct before the subject is reached. The middle stanza appears to reverse this order by closing its second-half stanza with a subordinate clause acting as adjunct. Other parallels, such as the two clauses in each half-stanza of the first stanza sharing the same subject, have been commented on in the analysis.

It is time now to consider the groups in the poem. It is a notable feature in it that the sentences, which are all declarative, are extremely short. It is unusual for a clause to run to more than two lines, and if it does so it is because it has a subordinate clause acting as adjunct attached to it. Even these subordinate clauses are short so that no complete clause runs to more than four lines. This naturally has an important bearing on the noun group, for as we saw earlier one way of making a sentence more elaborate was by extending the noun group. The fact that the sentences are short and lacking elaboration means that the noun groups are of necessity very brief. When we consider that a noun group can consist of determiner – modifier – head – qualifier, we realise what opportunities have been ignored by Auden. Only one noun group in this poem contains a qualifier despite the fact that qualifiers are so common in the language. This group *The loss of this* has a very short qualifier *of this* and can hardly have been included for purposes of elaboration. The central position of this line and group may suggest that within the poem it has a pivotal role. Very few groups contain modifiers either. The two modifiers which strike one immediately are those found, significantly enough, in the first and the last lines: *This lunar beauty* and *His endless look*. *Lunar* and *beauty* are both bisyllables with stress on the first element which create a rhythmical pattern for the poem. It may be worth noting that both noun groups have a determiner, *This* and *His*, which show assonance, but do not rhyme because the final consonant is different. Each noun group occupies the whole line and the one echoes the other. Another group with a modifier is *other time* (9). The other modifiers are of a different nature and even then there are only two of them, namely *the heart's changes* and *A ghost's endeavour*. In these the possessive form in *'s* acts as a kind of modifier. In both cases the expansion of the noun group by including a modifier means that the group occupies a whole line, though in the first case there is also an *And*. Otherwise the noun groups consist either of the head alone or of head and determiner. In the first stanza the determiner *no* is contrasted with *any* and *a*, but many noun groups have the head alone: *beauty*, *It* and *another*. Indeed, it is a feature of this poem that there are so many noun groups which have only a head, often formed by a pronoun. Even those heads which are formed by nouns often have no determiners associated with them, such as *beauty*, *daytime*, *time*, *ghost*, *love* and *sorrow*. The absence of determiners is significant for the feel of the poem. It is one of the features which gives a gnomic quality to it because so often nouns without a determiner are abstract or refer to classes or types rather than to individual members within that class. The absence of determiners in these noun groups contrasts with the noun groups formed with a pronoun head, because the latter seem to be very specific whereas the former are more general.

Like the noun group, the verb group is also marked by its simplicity, for most of the groups consist of a single word, the verb or head itself. The poem contains a single modal auxiliary form, *shall* (21), and one *has* auxiliary; no verb group has an extension. The verb forms are all in the third person singular, mostly in the present tense, because there is nothing personal through the use of first or second persons here. These features also suggest a proverbial quality on the poem which appears to deal with what is perpetually true and with facts and ideas rather than with people. Because there are only short noun groups, there is a high proportion of verbs for the number of words in the poem and in this respect Auden's poem differs profoundly from Shakespeare's Sonnet 129. In that poem we saw there were very elaborate noun groups which could extend over several lines and most of the impact made by the poem was through the ornateness of the groups.

In the first stanza there are five verbs, all consisting of the simple verb: *has*, *is*, *bear*, *had* and *is*. It is worth noting that the verbs themselves are relatively uncomplicated since *to be* and *to have* are among the commonest verbs in the language. *To be* is stative and *to have* dynamic, and the two examples of each are separated by *bear*, a dynamic verb. The form *bear* is an older subjunctive type within the conditional subordinate clause beginning with *If*. Apart from expressions like *If I were you*, it is today somewhat unusual to have the subjunctive form without *-s* in the third person singular. Most of us today say *If he comes tomorrow* rather than *If he come tomorrow*. When Auden wrote this poem in the 1930s it was still common in more formal

English to use the subjunctive in *If* clauses, but its use here does make the poem seem more distant. It counteracts any feeling of colloquialism which one might expect the shorter sentences to provide. The conditional clause with *bear* makes it difficult to interpret the *had* and *is* which follow. The conditional clause and its use of *later* indicate that the time sequence would be something in the future, yet the verb form *had* suggests that we have a time sequence in the past unless we also understand this verb to have a hypothetical sense of 'would have had' – a sense which seems difficult to justify with the *is* which follows, which would have to be understood as 'would be'. The hypothesis of the conditional *if* seems to produce something which is a fact, as much as to say that if *x* happens, then it follows that *y* must have happened and *z* is true. The condition can be fulfilled, it is suggested, only if other possibilities have in fact taken place and have established themselves as fact.

In the second stanza there are four verbs: *keeps, is, is* and *has*. We may note again the reappearance of the verbs *to have* and *to be*. Even the verb *keeps*, which might normally be thought of as dynamic, here has the feel of a verb which is less dynamic and more stative because it refers to something which appears to be always true rather than to something which is changing or developing. In the last verbal group we may assume for the moment that the sense is *has haunted lost and wanted*, in which *has* is the auxiliary for the three participial heads. It is a feature of all three verbs that they are normally transitive, that is they have an object, though in this poem none is used transitively. Each is used as though it is an intransitive verb, though it could be assumed that *heart's changes* is the object to these verbs. However, *where* which refers back to *heart's changes* is a relative of place. The absence of objects for these verbs does suggest something less tangible which contributes to the overall sense of unreality and timelessness in the poem.

The third stanza has five verbal groups: *was, was, pass, shall near* and (*shall*) *take*. Again we may note the frequency of the verb *to be*. In the first half-stanza there is also the participial form *finished* in the non-finite clause *finished this* meaning 'when this was finished'. In the second half-stanza *till* usually introduces a temporal clause, though in this case the use of the subjunctive introduces an element of the hypothetical into the clause suggesting condition as much as time. In this it is like the conditional *If* clause, but different from the *Where* clause which appears to be factual rather than hypothetical. The sense also suggests that the *till* may not indicate that it will pass, but only that it may pass; the passing is possible rather than definite. This *till* clause influences the meaning of the main clauses with *shall*. The *shall* has the older sense of obligation or definiteness. Until it pass, these other things have no possibility of happening for the *shall* makes it clear that this negation is very strong indeed.

Of other groups there are few and they have little effect on the structure of the poem. There are few single-word adjuncts like *later* and *here*, and there are the clause adjuncts like *later* and *here*, and there are the clause adjuncts introduced by *If*, *Where* and *till*. The absence of many adjuncts helps to maintain the proverbial tone, because what is stated is not seen to refer to a particular time or place, but it is universally valid. Even the clause adjuncts are hardly specific, since they mainly refer to what might happen.

It may be appropriate at this stage to consider the cohesion in the poem and to leave the vocabulary till later in the discussion. This is because cohesion is clearly an important element in it since the poem consists of short clauses which do not necessarily have much apparent interconnection. The opening of the poem, which is also its title, is *This lunar beauty* and appears to offer a form of exophoric cohesion since there is no immediate referent for *This*. What beauty is under discussion? Does the reader share the author's knowledge and know what *This lunar beauty* refers to? It is said to have *no history* and to be *complete and early*. Something which has *no history* is cohesively associated with completeness, because history implies change which could be seen as an antithesis of completeness. *Early* has a cohesiveness with history in a different way because something which is early, i.e. young, has no history because its history, or the way in which it changes and develops, has not yet begun. It is also possible to think of *lunar* as possibly having cohesion with *history* in so far as the moon is always there and is always the same even though it waxes and wanes. *Beauty*, however, can only be thought of as contrasting with *history*, since beauty is of its nature transient which is the opposite of having no history.

In line 4 there is a repetition of *beauty* which ties it to the first line. *Later* is cohesive to *early*, because these two represent opposite ends of a time sequence. Beauty is often thought to reside in features, and so there is some cohesion between *feature* and *beauty*. In line 6 *It* must refer to *beauty* and is a form of pronominal cohesion and as subject it is taken over to the clause in line 7. There is a natural link between *beauty* and *lover* since these are two words which are often linked together; beauty and love go hand in hand. In the second half-stanza there is reference to *beauty* as against *This lunar beauty*, and the former seems to be a generalisation of the latter. The *It* of line 6 refers back to *beauty* in line 4, but it is not evident whether both refer to *This lunar beauty* in line 1 or represent some broadening of that subject.

This matter is of some importance because when the second stanza starts it is introduced by *This*, which stands as a noun group by itself as the subject of the clause. Since it echoes the *This* in *This lunar beauty* at the beginning of the first stanza, one assumes that it is cohesive with that noun group rather than with *beauty*, which is actually closer to it. Also in line 1 the word *dream* is cohesive with *lunar*, because both moon and dreaming are associated with the night. The same may be said of *lover*, since loving and dreaming are often closely associated with each other. This link of dreaming and loving with lunar is accentuated by *daytime* in line 10, which stands in a contrastive relationship with these words: dreaming and lunar are associated with night. Daytime is said to be *the loss of this*, and the obvious link of *this* (11) with *This* (8) and *This lunar beauty* (1) indicates that daytime leads to the destruction of lunar beauty. In line 9 it is said to keep *other time*. *Other* echoes *another* but seems to be set in a contrastive relationship with it. Time is linked with history in so far as history records the passage of time in human affairs. The fact that lunar beauty has no history and keeps other time, i.e. other from that which is true of humans generally, links the two together even more closely. In line 12 *time* is repeated and links with *other time* in line 9. But the time which is mentioned here is apparently ordinary time and so has a contrastive relationship with other time, though the same word is used. The word *heart* in *heart's changes* has a cohesive link with *beauty* and *lover*, since love is often thought to be seated in the heart and love is in its turn associated with beauty. Change is linked with history, as we have seen in that history records the changes in human existence. In the following line *ghost* is introduced. This has a link with *lunar*, since the moon is thought of as ghostly and since it is in the moonlight that ghosts are most usually encountered. *Ghost* is linked with *haunted* since it is ghosts which haunt houses or people. *Lost* is linked with *the loss of this* and this link suggests that there may be some association between lines 14–15 and lines 10–11. *Daytime* is contrastive with *ghost* since it is at night that ghosts are wont to haunt. If daytime is the loss of this and if time is where ghost has haunted and lost, then ghost and lunar beauty may be both lost when time is human rather than other time. Ghost is also said to have *wanted*. This may have some link with *lover* and even *dream*, both of which imagine things which are desired, but the link can hardly be thought of as very strong.

The third stanza starts almost in the same way as the second, except it has *But* before *this*. Once again one has to ask what *this* relates to. Inevitably one assumes that it is the same as *This* (8) and *This lunar beauty* (1), but in this stanza the link is complicated by a further *this* in line 18: *finished this*. This second *this* is said to be finished and that suggests change. Consequently both *this* of line 16 and *this* of line 18 appear to suggest something which could change like the time of line 12. If they refer to beauty or lunar beauty, it suggests that both can and do change. There is one form of beauty which does not change and another which can and does. It is possible to assume that each *this* in the third stanza refers to something different and that they are not parallel but opposed. The *this* in line 18 certainly seems to refer to lunar beauty, the end of which would make the ghost uncomfortable or unhappy. If so, the *this* of line 16 could be the changes wrought by time, for it was never ghost's endeavour to bring about changes and when they do come ghost is distressed. This in many ways seems the most satisfactory solution. A *ghost's endeavour* is presumably related to *haunting* since that is what a ghost does. Hence where the ghost has haunted in the heart's changes is not the same as his attempt to create those changes. The *it* of line 20 may refer to *this* (18), for *pass* as a verb refers both to *finished*, because when something has passed it is finished, and earlier to *time* and *changes*, because for anything to pass involves changes over time. The whole clause *till it pass* is linked with the earlier subordinate clause *If beauty later/ Bear any feature*, because both refer to the potential passing and changing of beauty. *Love* in line 21 naturally coheres with *lover* (6) and with the words which existed in cohesion with it. The verb *near* (21), which has the sense of 'approach', stands in contrast to *pass* (20), which has the sense of disappearing or of going further away. In line 22 *sweetness* is linked to *love*, because love and sweetness go together. In the same line *here* is associated with *near*, because both are concerned with what is close to the speaker, and it stands in an opposed relation to *pass*, which is associated with the opposite of *here*, namely *there*. There is a natural contrast between *sorrow* (23) and *Sweetness* (22), though sorrow might also be said to have a link with love since love can often be unhappy when it is unrequited or when it passes. The verb *take* (23) has a possible contrast with *lost*, because what is taken is acquired as against what has been lost. In the following line *endless* is naturally associated with *time*, for time is endless. It is also linked with *no history* (2) because anything which has no history could also be said to be timeless and so endless. The final word *look* has some link with *feature*, because looks and features are not too far apart in meaning. *Look* is also connected with *beauty*, since beauty is regularly said to lie in the eye of the beholder.

The poem is very densely textured in its cohesion. Although it seems to be a simple and uncomplicated poem, it has many devices which link with other parts of the poem and provide a tautly knit structure. There is progression as represented by the increase in length of each stanza, but there is also stability represented by the cohesion. This duality is something which we also need to consider in the vocabulary, though some of the semantic links have already been indicated through the discussion of cohesion.

Although the poem appears to be uncomplicated in that it consists of very short clauses in a semi-proverbial style, the vocabulary itself is not as Anglo-Saxon as one might expect. It is true that there are few words of three syllables which one might expect to find in a piece of ornate writing. Even those words of three syllables that exist, *history* and *endeavour*, are not unusual words as such, though both are learned and Latinate. There are many words of two syllables, many of which are also Latinate or have come into English from Latin through French. In the first stanza alone, apart from *history* there are the following Latinate words: *lunar*, *beauty*, *complete* and *feature*. The most important of these is *lunar*, since it may be thought to be the key to the poem appearing as it does in the poem's first line and its title. The word was borrowed into English in the seventeenth century and is an adjective from the Latin *luna* 'the moon'. The moon has various associations attached to it in Latin and in English. It affects people's behaviour as suggested by the word *lunatic*; it is transient but permanent at the same time; it is eerie because it encourages unusual behaviour; it is beautiful and almost magical; and it represents something intangible, though visible. A phrase like *lunar beauty* could mean the beauty of the moon or it may imply a beauty which has characteristics of those we otherwise associate with the moon. In this case since there seems to be no further reference to the moon or extra-terrestial bodies, the second meaning appears to be predominant. What or who is beautiful is not stated, because beauty is regarded in the poem as something in its own right. But lunar beauty could be something which is beautiful in an almost supernatural way, perhaps even slightly fey, because although potentially permanent it seems susceptible to change. *Lunar* may suggest something wistful because of its apparent unreality in that moonlight is only a pale reflection of sunlight. It is this word which sets the tone for the rest of the poem particularly in its suggestion of a desire for permanence together with a recognition of change. The association of the moon with magic is another important force here. *Lunar* is used metaphorically because the poem is not about the moon and this is one of the few words in the poem for which a metaphoric sense is clear. It is in fact often said that Auden wrote this poem when he was a schoolmaster and he was inspired to write this poem by looking at a photograph of one of the boys at the school. But there is nothing personal or individual about the poem, and the Latinate vocabulary of this first stanza helps to achieve a generalising sense which the poet evidently wants to get across.

Beauty when used with a determiner such as *this* would normally be a count noun and have the sense of a particular beauty or person; without a determiner as in line 4 it would imply the abstract qualities which go to make up beauty. Auden amalgamates the two so that we are not clear which one is in question, because he wants us to consider a particular example of beauty to represent beauty as a collection of abstract qualities. *History* is a word with learned associations partly because of the academic subject and partly because of its link with writing. Because history is the written record of what has happened, this lunar beauty which has no history appears to exist outside that record and this is what makes it seem insubstantial. If something exists outside history it exists to some extent outside time, just as to some extent the moon does or at least was thought to do. *Complete* is another Latinate word, usually meaning 'entire, finished'. It also has other meanings, some of which are somewhat archaic, but which may be invoked by Auden. Anything which is entire and finished can be thought of as perfect or without blemish and hence even to be consummate, senses which are inherent in the title of Izaak Walton's book *The Compleat Angler*. These senses are not inappropriate here and could well be implied. *Early* is another word which may be used in a slightly less common sense because it suggests not so much early in time as early in age. Hence there is a sense of youthful innocence, a sense which goes well enough with *lunar*. There is a contrast between these two words for something which is perfectly entire is hardly likely to be in the first age which is when things are under formation. Both *complete* and *early* have favourable connotations which relate well to *beauty*.

In line 5 there are two words, *bear* and *feature*, which deserve comment. *Feature* is also a word of Latin origin and has two meanings which might be relevant here. The first is 'shape, form' and the second is 'the lineaments of the face, the form of its parts'. Either of these suggest that beauty is something abstract which exists separate from its material form which it can adopt. The two senses suggest also that beauty can be seen either as an individual or more generally as something in nature. The verb *bear* has the sense of 'wear, carry' and is now somewhat archaic in the sense of wearing an expression or facial feature. If the word is used today it is perhaps most often associated with bearing a burden, either literally or metaphorically, and that might well be implied here since beauty in taking any feature is bearing a burden. In the sense of 'wear' which is predominant here the verb is archaic, and this word, with the Latinate ones, helps to create the distancing effect of this poem. The distancing is accentuated by the employment of the subjunctive without -*s*. Although it may have originated in a real experience, it portrays what appears to be a general situation expressed in terms which are proverbial and non-specific. The word *lover* (6) is connotatively linked with the male sex, though that connotation is now less strong than it was. Since *beauty* is often linked with the female sex connotatively, the linking of *lover* and *beauty* does suggest that there might be a sexual implication here of the love of a male for a female. However, this beauty is later and different, *is another* (7), from that described in the first half-stanza which appears to be without the associations of sex and maturity which is why the feeling of innocence suggested by *early* and *lunar* are intensified by the words which follow.

The second stanza differs from the first in using words which are all monosyllabic and usually of Anglo-Saxon origin. Some of the words have two syllables because of the use of inflexional endings, *inches* and *changes* for example, and one word, *daytime*, is a compound though it is formed from two simple monosyllabic Anglo-Saxon words. These words contribute to the proverbial tone of this stanza, though it is interesting that the stanza which has the most syntactic complexity has the least ornate vocabulary. Some of the statements are almost gnomic, such as *Time is inches*, which is metaphorical for the concept that time can be measured by the number of inches a young person grows over the years. It is possible that *inches and heart's changes* may be thought of as a hendiadys, meaning the 'inch by inch changes in the heart', but this seems improbable. *Ghost* is not normally a non-count noun, but its use as such contributes to the sense of generalising which is so characteristic of the poem.

The third stanza is more like the first in having some polysyllabic vocabulary; only one word contains three syllables, *endeavour*, though several contain two, *finished*, *sweetness*, *sorrow* and *endless*. All these bisyllabic words are linked in some way. *Finished* is the opposite to *endless*, *endless* itself rhymes with *sweetness*, and *sweetness* contrasts with *sorrow*. Apart from *finished* these words are of Anglo-Saxon origin. Perhaps *near* is the most unusual word since it is used as a verb rather than as an adverb, which is its normal usage. But even so it does not create an out-of-the-way effect because the word is otherwise so common and the functional shift so easy. *Endeavour*, *finish* and *ease* are all of French origin in English, but all have been in the language a long time and hardly seem foreign to most speakers of the language. *Endeavour* is hardly a word which seems appropriate to a ghost because it suggests making an effort and striving, and ghosts being insubstantial hardly have the capability to undertake anything which needs effort. *Ease* might well be associated with ghosts since they are often thought to need propitiation in order to cease their haunting, as is implied by the ghost in *Hamlet*. Only when they have been able to get redemption or achieve some form of revenge can they achieve peace and stop haunting. Indeed, ghosts are traditionally thought of as unhappy and restless, and so words like *endless*, *sorrow* and not being *at ease* fit well with this general scenario. However, none of the words in this stanza are sufficiently unusual to call attention to themselves, and they blend together well to create the tone of something which has been lost and which can never be recaptured. The vocabulary fits in well with the elements of cohesion found in the poem.

In an earlier chapter I looked at pragmatics in relation to a piece of dramatic writing which resembles ordinary conversation. Clearly that kind of approach cannot be applied to poetry so readily because of its different nature. It may be easiest to start a consideration of pragmatics in relation to poetry by looking at deixis, a feature that we hardly bothered to examine in any detail in *Hamlet*. 'This Lunar Beauty' has no first or second person personal pronouns. Indeed, it is noticeable that it has few pronoun subjects at all: *it* is used twice. It does have one possessive pronoun form, *his*, referring to *sorrow*, and it has many examples of *this*, either as adjective or as pronoun. Because there are no first and second person forms, we assume that the poem is uttered by someone who is addressing the world in general rather than a particular person. The individual who is uttering the poem and the person to whom it could be addressed are not significant apparently and are subsumed within the general nature of the poem itself. It is necessary to write 'apparently' because the use of *this* in the opening line and elsewhere does create a conversational tone which suggests one person speaking to another. One has only to compare the language of Sonnet 129 to understand this point. There the subjects are abstracts such as *TH'expence of Spirit* and *lust*, or generalising forms such as *the world* and *none*. But when a poem opens *This lunar beauty*, it suggests that there is a speaker and a listener, who both share the knowledge inherent in that *this* because there is no explanation of it later in the poem. It is not cataphoric; it is exophoric, for it refers to something outside the poem. Hence the tone of the poem is one of shared knowledge and potential intimacy, because writer and reader are assumed to be familiar with the topic being discussed. This method of writing is one which is much commoner in modern poetry and helps to create a conversational tone in dealing with a subject that is apparently general and almost didactic.

This more intimate tone is further developed by other adjuncts and by the use of count nouns as though they were non-count ones. One adjunct which has potential deictic implications is *here* (22). This can be interpreted as a general adjunct meaning something like 'in this world', or it could mean 'in the place associated with the lunar beauty and the writer of the poem'. If the latter, which seems perhaps the more satisfactory, then the reference is anaphoric and can be understood within terms of the poem itself, though it does imply that the reader knows where this *here* is and so assumes some shared knowledge again. Another adjunct which could be deictic is *later* (4). This can also be explained in terms of the poem as meaning 'later than the time we are talking about, in the future'. In line 4 *beauty* is introduced as a non-count noun, although in line 1 *This lunar beauty* indicates that *beauty* as a count noun refers to one specific example of beauty. The example of beauty in line 4 can be understood as referring back to this particular beauty in line 1 and would then be a less formal way of making a second reference to it, almost as though *beauty* were almost a pet-name for *This lunar beauty*. Naturally, it also has the advantage that it can be understood as referring to beauty as an abstract entity which is wider than *This lunar beauty* even if it embraces it. In lines 14 and 19 *ghost* is introduced as a non-count noun, though it is usually a count noun in English. The effect is less general than *a ghost* would be, but perhaps less clear than *the ghost*. In a strange way it suggests that writer and reader share some knowledge that explains what this ghost or even ghostly quality might be, even though it is not explained in the poem. The two entities *beauty* and *ghost* balance each other and suggest some interaction between them which is known to the reader of the poem.

In discussing the opening of *Hamlet* we considered the presuppositions which lay behind the various utterances; this approach we can now apply to this poem though it may not be so easy to come to firm conclusions. The opening clauses in lines 1–3 present some of the difficulties inherent in the approach and the interpretation of the poem. To say that a lunar beauty has no history and is complete and early suggests that a lunar beauty should have some history and should not be complete and early. This is the implication of *This*, because it apparently distinguishes a specific lunar beauty from other lunar beauties. This assumption seems to be justified by the claim in line 7 that beauty could be *another*, i.e. that it could be different by having a history and not being complete and early. In Sonnet 129 the absence of determiners like *this* makes us assume that what is being spoken about, *lust in action*, is universally true; but in Auden's poem we appear to be considering a single example of lunar beauty which is presented through *This*. So the presupposition is that lunar beauty has a history and the author is here explaining to the reader that this particular example is different. The conversational tone supports this presupposition behind the poem. It is accentuated by the absence of an expressed subject of the second clause, for *This lunar beauty* must be the subject of this clause as well. But the absence of the subject creates a presupposition of intimacy between writer and reader because the grammar is telescoped in this way. The rest of this stanza presupposes that it is normal for beauty to have features and consequently to have a lover and be different from this lunar beauty. It appears to establish what might be the norms expected, from which the subject of this poem differs. It establishes the uniqueness of the beauty which is the subject under discussion. What is not made explicit is how this beauty differs from the norm or why, and more importantly what form this particular beauty takes. That appears to be knowledge which the reader should have available or which has to be assumed is less important.

In the second stanza it is said that *This . . . keeps other time*. Presumably it is the same lunar beauty which keeps other time. The presupposition is that most things keep to historical time, whereas this lunar beauty lies outside historical time. Hence it is like a dream, for that also is timeless or exists outside time. The reference to dream fixes this other time to be something which is either immutable or outside time. It is lost when day comes. Although day is opposite to dreaming and to lunar, which is why it destroys both dreams and lunar beauty, the lunar beauty which is the subject of the poem is not apparently linked immediately to the moon since the moon is changing and is part of time. We accept some metaphorical extension here where lunar beauty refers to a form of beauty which is 'moonlike' perhaps, but which is not actually of the moon. By 'moonlike' we may well understand something chaste, pure, white and innocent. The statement that time is inches and the heart's changes is not one that makes sense immediately unless we presuppose that this is metaphorical in expression. Time can be measured through growth as represented by inches, which must mean animal or plant growth, and through the changes in the heart, which must mean the development in human emotional responses represented by the heart. Since such emotional responses are characteristic only of humans, we presuppose that the inches also refer to human growth. The presupposition is that as we grow older so we change our emotional attitudes, whereas the lunar beauty which is outside this time shows no changes in growth or emotions. It must be frozen at some point in its development to show no change. One such frozen point in human growth is precisely a photograph which never changes and never grows. The last two lines of this stanza refer to *Where ghost has haunted/ Lost and wanted*. It is perhaps immaterial whether the *Where* refers to time or to the heart, since the two are related. We may assume that ghost is also metaphorical here since ghosts do not inhabit hearts and are not essentially part of time. It appears to represent what the heart tries to achieve emotionally, something which is insubstantial but which is nevertheless strongly desired. *Lost* and *wanted* are placed in an order which is not that which one might expect since wanting normally precedes losing. It may suggest a certain dislocation in the continuity of the cycle of wanting and losing, for it happens continually in time; it is not something which occurs only once and that partly explains the sorrow of the heart's changes. It is not part of a ghost's haunting that it should be associated with losing and wanting, and this is why we presupose a metaphorical meaning here. The ghost within the heart has emotions or is the personified emotion.

The presuppositions which lie behind the opening lines of the final stanza are difficult to assess, because the behaviour which a ghost might follow is not something which forms part of our everyday experience. Yet the double occurrence of *this* maintains the tone of intimacy between writer and reader. There is an assumption that ghosts do try to achieve something, and that we would normally understand as being the achievement of revenge or something similar. Ghosts try to do this in order to achieve rest so that they no longer need to haunt the humans who are left behind in this world. Hence if a ghost finishes its endeavour, it would normally expect to find peace or to be at ease. Then in line 20 there is reference to *till it pass*, but the referent of *it* is not explicit. It could be either *this* or *ghost's endeavour*. Since the verb *pass* implies change, *it* may even refer to *time* from the previous stanza. One final possibility is that it refers to *ghost*, though we tend perhaps to anthropomorphise ghosts if we can, because ghosts are normally associated with dead human beings. In the final part of the stanza we presuppose that love is sweetness and sorrow is endless, but that neither of these qualities can operate unless certain conditions are met. The primary condition is being human, for with humans there is time and that implies change.

The final aspect of pragmatics considered in our earlier chapter concerned the co-operative principle and the syntactic means used to give expression to it. Naturally as the poem contains no dialogue, the co-operative principle can hardly be invoked. We have already noted that each clause is declarative and the poem works essentially on the basis of making statements one after the other. Because there is no elaboration at clause or group level, these statements follow in an order which is progressive. Although the poem may be a description of a photograph, that is not the subject as such. The subject is rather a series of reflections arising from a consideration of a particular form of beauty and this leads the author to describe his reaction to the reader in a way which suggests that they share many of the same assumptions about the topic. The original picture of beauty leads through to some moral conclusions after a review of the difference between the type of beauty represented and that which we all regard as characteristic of human life. The views of the author are presented as though they are universally valid, though the author through his choice of linguistic structures is able to assume that his reader is with him on this intellectual journey. The author does not try to elaborate on his theme by an form of poetic ornamentation and to that extent he does not flout the maxim of quantity or even necessarily quality. Each statement proceeds in a sequence and each builds upon the position arrived at in the last. The poem is not a static description, as Shakespeare's Sonnet 129 is.

Throughout this chapter I have taken the main points of

analysis outlined in each preceding chapter in this book and applied them in turn to a single poem. It may well seem as though this leads to critical overkill. But the point of this chapter has been to show how these various techniques can be applied so that a given poem can be appreciated more fully and critically. Inevitably how much of stylistic analysis any reader will need to do will depend partly on that reader's critical and stylistic experience, partly on what the analysis is needed for and partly on the complexity of the poem under consideration. But all the different facets of stylistic analysis yield some profit, as I hope this book has made clear, and even the simplest poem can be made to offer unexpected insights through their application. It is now up to you, the readers, to experience this widening of your critical responses for yourselves. Good luck!

Notes

INTRODUCTION

1 Michael Cummings and Robert Simmons, *The Language of Literature: A Stylistic Introduction to the Study of Literature* (Oxford: Pergamon, 1983), p. xv.
2 Antony Easthope, *Poetry as Discourse* (London: Methuen, 1983), p. 8.
3 Roman Jakobson and Lawrence G. Jones, *Shakespeare's Verbal Art in Th'Expence of Spirit*, De Proprietatibus Litterarum series practica 35 (The Hague: Mouton, 1970).
4 M.A.K. Halliday, 'Linguistic Function and Literary Style: An Inquiry into the Language of William Golding's "The Inheritors"', in Donald C. Freeman (ed.), *Essays in Modern Stylistics* (London and New York: Methuen, 1981), pp. 325–60.
5 N. F. Blake, *Traditional English Grammar and Beyond* (Basingstoke: Macmillan, 1988).

1 SENTENCE STRUCTURE

1 From now on the following abbreviations may be used:
S = subject; P = predicator; O = object; C = complement; A = adjunct.

3 GROUP STRUCTURE: THE OTHER GROUPS

1 Halliday, 'Linguistic Function and Literary Style'.

Suggestions for Further Reading

The linguistic background necessary for appreciating the language of literature can be acquired from N. F. Blake, *Traditional English Grammar and Beyond* (Macmillan, 1988); Dennis Freeborn, *A Course Book in English Grammar* (Macmillan, 1987); or Geoffrey Leech, Margaret Deuchar and Robert Hoogenraad, *English Grammar for Today: A New Introduction* (Macmillan, 1982). A more advanced grammar is M.A.K. Halliday, *An Introduction to Functional Grammar* (Arnold, 1985).

General introductions to stylistics can be found in A. Cluysenaar, *Introduction to Literary Stylistics* (Batsford, 1976); M. Cummings and R. Simmons, *The Language of Literature: A Stylistic Introduction to the Study of Literature* (Pergamon, 1983); A. Easthope, *Poetry as Discourse* (Methuen, 1983); R. Fowler, *Linguistic Criticism* (Oxford University Press, 1986); and E. Closs Traugott and Mary Louise Pratt, *Linguistics for Students of Literature* (Harcourt Brace Jovanovich, 1980).

Collections of essays on stylistics are edited in R. A. Carter, *Language and Literature: An Introductory Reader in Stylistics* (Allen & Unwin, 1982); R. A. Carter and P. Simpson, *Language, Discourse and Literature* (Unwin Hyman, 1989); Donald C. Freeman, *Linguistics and Literary Style* (Holt, Rinehart & Winston, 1970); and Donald C. Freeman, *Essays in Modern Stylistics* (Methuen, 1981).

Approaches to particular types of literature can be found in G. Leech, *A Linguistic Guide to English Poetry* (Longman, 1969); G. Leech and M. Short, *Style in Fiction. A Linguistic Guide to English Fictional Prose* (Longman, 1981); and R. Fowler, *Linguistics and the Novel* (Methuen, 1977).

A useful introduction to lexis is Ronald Carter, *Vocabulary* (Allen & Unwin, 1987).

For sound, metre and rhetoric consult Derek Attridge, *The Rhythms of English Poetry* (Longman, 1982); Raymond Chapman, *The Treatment of Sounds in Language and Literature* (Blackwell, 1984); and Brian Vickers, *Classical Rhetoric in English Poetry* (Macmillan, 1970).

Two good introductions to cohesion are Waldemar Gutwinski, *Cohesion in Literary Texts: A Study of Some Grammatical and Lexical Features of*

English Discourse (Mouton, 1974); and M.A.K. Halliday and Ruqaiya Hasan, *Cohesion in English* (Longman, 1976).

For pragmatics and discourse see Gillian Brown and George Yule, *Discourse Analysis* (Cambridge University Press, 1983); Geoffrey Leech, *The Principles of Pragmatics* (Longman, 1983); Stephen C. Levison, *Pragmatics* (Cambridge University Press, 1983); and Mary Louise Pratt, *Towards a Speech Act Theory of Literary Discourse* (Indiana University Press, 1976).

For a general account of the interaction of language and literary critical theory see David Birch, *Language, Literature and Critical Practice: Ways of Analysing Text* (Routledge, 1989). There is now a dictionary of stylistic terms available in Katie Wales, *A Dictionary of Stylistics* (Longman, 1989).

Index